Blackson Makhumba B

THE PERSONAL WORK
A Handbook for a Christian Worker

"The harvest truly is great, but the laborers are few: pray ye therefore the Lord of the harvest, that he would send forth laborers to his harvest" -- Luke 10:2

The Personal Work:
A Handbook for a Christian Worker
Copyright © Divine Charisma Books
Copyright © 2015Divine Charisma Books

Published By Parables

All rights reserved solely by the author. The author guarantees all contents are original and do not infringe upon the legal rights of any other person or work. No part of this book may be reproduced in any form without the permission of the author. The views expressed in this book are not necessarily those of the publisher.
First Edition   June, 2017

ISBN978-1-945698-21-7

Readers should be aware that Internet Web sites offered as citations and/or sources for further information may have been changed or disappeared between the time this was written and when it is read.

Cover, Layout and Design by Andrew Deba and Dr. B. Makhumba, Divine Charisma Book and Graphic Designers- Cell: +265885207370, +265881004309

E-Mail: charismadivine@gmail.com
Website; www.divine-charisma.webnode.com

Blackson Makhumba B

THE PERSONAL WORK
A Handbook for a Christian Worker

"The harvest truly is great, but the laborers are few: pray ye therefore the Lord of the harvest, that he would send forth laborers to his harvest" -- Luke 10:2

PUBLISHED by PARABLES
Earthly Stories with a Heavenly Meaning

ACKNOWLEDGEMENT

First, all praises be to the Lord Jesus for His goodness and mercies everlasting. To my virtuous wife, Nyamtegha for allowing me to use much of time meant for you. Our blessed three rising stars (Agape, Melchizedek and Comfort, the Prophetess); I do not debase your presence and noise contribution. You guys Rock

Lastly, I acknowledge the timely contributions, in various forms, of the following friends: Bishop and Mama Ben Sibakwe, Pastors G. Phiri (Adaliska), Jean Sauti Phiri, Crosby Kamanga, Justine Mpira, Elder Brino Kumwenda (Radio ABC), and every one of you who has helped to make this book possible, you are too numerous to mention. We succeed together.

BLACKSON MAKHUMBA B

DEDICATION

I wholeheartedly dedicate this book to my spiritual father and friend, Reverend Richard Mongola Chirwa, and to my friend indeed and in need Blester Mara. I do not forget your affable contribution to my life, and that of my family. You deserve a gift more than this.

TABLE OF CONTENTS

1. The Basis Of Personal Work — 12
2. Importance of Personal Work — 22
3. Qualifications Of A Christian Worker — 30
4. All Should Work — 37
5. Soul-Winning — 44
6. Principles Of Soul-Winning — 51
7. Where, When & How — 56
8. The Follow-Up — 66
9. Ministering To Backsliders — 74
10. Answering Doubts And Excuses — 83

THE PERSONAL WORK

11. Dealing With Skeptics And Infidels	91
12. Muhammad, Islam & Qur'an	98
13. Evangelizing To The Muslim Brother	106
14. Dealing With Jehovah's Witnesses	118
15. Biblical Texts For The Deity Of Christ	130
16. Dealing With Mormons	137
17. Facts And Evidence Against Mormons	143
18. Evangelizing To The Roman Catholicist	152
19. Tips For A Personal Worker	163
Primary Source References	172

1
THE BASIS OF PERSONAL WORK

Sometimes a personal worker is known as a 'Christian worker' or a 'Church worker' depending on the context. In this book, these three terms are used interchangeably to mean the same thing. This is so because a worker can be a pastor, missionary, an evangelist, and church planters or any church leader working on special program. It may also mean any person giving a helping hand to the church leadership in carrying out God's work.

The Global Gospel Network Ministries suggest three definitions for a Christian worker basing on Numbers chapter 11:

The Personal Work

1. *A Christian worker is a helping hand to the church leader* (Num.11:17)

2. *A Christian worker is a person called to help share the leader's responsibilities* (Num. 11:17)

3. *It is a person who can possess the same Spirit as of the leader and leads a yielded life* (Num.11:25).

According to today's church setting, all the above definitions limit the Christian work to those working under certain leadership, excluding leaders themselves. It only considers local church workers like deacons, administrators, intercession leaders, praise team leaders and others. However, the wider concept of Christian worker goes beyond these lines. It includes both leaders and those serving under them. In fact, it involves every member of the body of Christ. Each of us has a role to play.

In this case I define a Christian worker in a much more generalized form: *A Christian worker is a person called by God, and has responded positively and is committed, to do a specified work or ministry for Christ.* This includes any persons working for God including the apostles, prophets, teachers, pastors, evangelists, usher etc.

Every true born again person is called upon to be a worker for God. We are not saved to sit and soak, but to serve. The Bible condemns idleness and calls it 'sin'. We are constantly exhorted to be busy just like Christ was busy. Too many Christians today do not follow the example of Christ.

A. The Mandate

Christian work is not based on human inkling, but it is biblical mandate.. The Bible has several passages on the reasons for Christian workers. For example, Romans 12:3-8 is one unique passage for the need of Christian workers. Each one of us has a gift to serve with. The Bible commands to do Christian work. Thus, we are fulfilling the Great Commission. Below are only few of these scriptural passages working as the basis for Christian work:

Mark 16:15-20: "And he said unto them, Go ye into the entire world, and preach the gospel to every creature. He that believeth and is baptized shall be saved; but he that believeth not shall be damned. And these signs shall follow them that believe; in my name shall they cast out devils; they shall speak with new tongues; they shall take up serpents; and if they drink any deadly thing, it shall not hurt them; they shall lay hands on the sick, and they shall recover. So then after the Lord had spoken unto them, he was received up into heaven, and sat on the right hand of God. And they went forth, and preached everywhere, the Lord working with them, and confirming the word with signs following. Amen"

Mt. 28:19-28: "Go ye therefore, and teach all nations, baptizing them in the name of the Father, and of the Son, and of the Holy Ghost: Teaching them to observe all things whatsoever I have commanded you: and, lo, I am with you always, even unto the end of the world. Amen"

Luke. 24:46-53: "And said unto them, thus it is written, and thus it behoved Christ to suffer and to rise from the dead the third day: And that repentance and remission of sins should be preached in his name among all nations, beginning at Jerusalem. And ye are witnesses of these things. And, behold, I send the promise of my Father upon you: but tarry ye in the city of Jerusalem, until ye be endued with power from on high. …And were continually in the temple, praising and blessing God. Amen"

Acts 1:8: "But ye shall receive power, after that the Holy Ghost is come upon you: and ye shall be witnesses unto me both in Jerusalem, and in all Judaea, and in Samaria, and unto the uttermost part of the earth."

Acts 8:4: "Therefore they that were scattered abroad went everywhere preaching the word".

2 Tim.2:15: "Study to shew thyself approved unto God, a workman that needeth not to be ashamed, rightly dividing the Word of Truth"

1 Pet.3:15: "But sanctify the Lord God in your hearts: and be ready always to give an answer to every man that asketh you a reason of the hope that is in you with meekness and fear"

2 Tim.4:2: "Preach the Word; be instant in

season, out of season; reprove, rebuke, exhort with all longsuffering and doctrine"

Isa.55:10-11: "For as the rain cometh down, and the snow from heaven, and returned not thither, but watereth the earth, and maketh it bring forth and bud, that it may give seed to the sower, and bread to the eater: So shall my word be that goeth forth out of my mouth: it shall not return unto me void, but it shall accomplish that which I please, and it shall prosper in the thing whereto I sent it"

Mt. 13:19-23: "When any one heareth the word of the kingdom, and understandeth it not… is he which received seed by the way side. But he that received the seed into stony places, the same is he that heareth the word, and anon with joy receiveth it; Yet hath he not root in himself, but dureth for a while: for when tribulation or persecution ariseth because of the word, by and by he is offended. He also that received seed among the thorns is he that heareth the word; and the care of this world, and the deceitfulness of riches, choke the word, and he became unfruitful. But he that received seed into the good ground is he that heareth the word, and understandeth it; which also beareth fruit, and bringeth forth, some an hundredfold, some sixty, some thirty"

Heb. 4:12: "For the word of God is quick, and powerful, and sharper than any two edged sword, piercing even to the dividing asunder of soul and spirit, and of the joints and marrow, and is a discerner of the thoughts and intents of the heart"

Prov.11:30: "The fruit of the righteous is a tree of life; and he that winneth souls is wise".

Daniel 12:3: "And they that are wise shall shine as the brightness of the firmament; and they that turn many to righteousness as the stars forever and ever"

B. Division of Labor

Perhaps the division of labor in Christian work at a local church is best described in these two passages:

Rom.12:3-8: *"For I say, through the grace given unto me, to every man that is among you, not to think of himself more highly than he ought to think; but to think soberly, according as God hath dealt to every man*

The Personal Work

the measure of faith. For as we have many members in one body, and all members have not the same office: So we, being many, are one body in Christ, and every one members one of another. Having then gifts differing according to the grace that is given to us, whether prophecy, let us prophesy according to the proportion of faith; Or ministry, let us wait on our ministering: or he that teacheth, on teaching; Or he that exhorteth, on exhortation: he that giveth, let him do it with simplicity; he that ruleth, with diligence; he that sheweth mercy, with cheerfulness"

Apostle Paul is explaining that all Christians make up one body in Christ, who is the Head of the body, and the common Centre of their unity. In the spiritual body, some are fitted for and called to one sort of work; others for another sort of work. Each one of us can do better where others cannot, but to the glory of God. We cannot all be pastor, evangelist, music director, Sunday school teacher, usher or usherette etc. We operate in different offices as the body parts operate. The leg is as useful as the head is, or as the finger. We are to do all the good we can, one to another, and for the common benefit.

Every Christian must attend on that calling wherein he is placed. Whatever our gifts or situations may be, let us try to employ ourselves humbly, diligently, cheerfully, and in simplicity; not seeking our own credit or profit, but the good of many, for this world and that which is to come.

Eph.4:7-13: *"But unto every one of us is given grace according to the measure of the gift of Christ. Wherefore he saith, when he ascended up on high, he led captivity captive, and gave gifts unto men. (Now that he ascended, what is it but that he also descended first into the lower parts of the earth? He that descended is the same also that ascended up far above all heavens, that he might fill all things.) And he gave some, apostles; and some, prophets; and some, evangelists; and some, pastors and teachers; For the perfecting of the saints, for the work of the ministry, for the edifying of the body of Christ: Till we all come in the unity of the faith, and of the knowledge of the Son of God, unto a perfect man, unto the measure of the stature of the fullness of Christ"*

Here the Apostle is emphasizing the fact that to every Christian is given some gift according to the measure to need, for mutual help.

The Personal Work

The fullness of each gift comes from one Lord Jesus Christ, and from one Holy Spirit and one God, even our Father. Each one's gift is unique and befitting for the kingdom growth. We all contribute to the proper functioning of the body.

2.
Importance of Personal Work

1. Why Does the Church Need Workers?
There are several reasons why the church needs workers, some of which are the following:

1. The church needs workers because we are all members of one body (1 Cor.12:12, 14, 20, 27). Therefore, each member of the body of Christ contributes to the proper functioning of the body (Eph.4; 16).

2. The Church needs workers because the church is God's visible manifestation of His kingdom to which all of us are its representatives (2 Cor. 5:20, 8:23).

3. The church needs workers because the work is more than one person can execute. (Exod. 18:13-18). Moses needed leaders over thousands, hundreds, fifties and over tens.

4. The church need workers because every living vision needs to be shared with others in order to be fulfilled (Heb.2:2, Isa.29:11-12, Ps.68:11). The Law was given to one man Moses on the Mountain, but he shred it to thousands of them, who later published or executed it. So too, Habakkuk had to write the vision, others had to read and run with it (Hab.2:2)

5. The church needs workers because our Lord Jesus Christ, the Head of the church designed and commenced the work as teamwork (Mat.4:18-22). Jesus called the twelve, trained them, and gave them the responsibility to minister (Lk. 9:1-2, 10:1-2).

6. The church needs workers because the apostles started and grew the church with workers (Acts 6:1-7, 14:21-23). The Apostles understood the importance of a shared responsibility.

Important: The main objective enveloping all the above reasons for every calling and ministry given to each believer is for equipping the saints for the service, and for proclaiming the Gospel of redemption to the entirety of the world, and for spiritual building up of the Church to maturity that can only be attained by proper Faith in the finished work of our Lord Jesus Christ.

Examples of Personal Works

As earlier said, Christian work include a variety of activities done on both local church and on a wider range basis. This is where one does a work of teaching the people, interpreting the scripture to them, and shows them the truth about the word of God within the community (community). This may include the following activities /ministries:

1. Personal evangelism (Jn. 1:36-51, 3:1-13, Acts 8:26-40, 9:17, 13:6-13)
2. Teaching, preaching, and healing work (Mat. 4:23-25)
3. Prison ministry (Acts 16:25-35)
4. Cottage, lodges or hotel ministry (Mt.3:14-18, Mk. 2:1-12, Acts 2:42-47)
5. Prayer meeting work (Acts 3:1, 4:23-31)

6. Bible school ministry (Acts 19:9-10, 2 kings 6)
7. Open air meeting evangelism (Mt.5:1, 24:3, Acts 16:12-13)
8. Pastoral, Missionary, and evangelistic work (Mt.16:15-20, 28:19-23)
9. Charity work (Romans 12:8)

2. Advantages of Personal Work over any other Christian ministry

Personal work has much advantage in that it is the easiest way of winning souls. For example, Apostles Peter and Nathaniel were brought to Jesus by the hand-to-hand work of his brother Andrew and Phillip respectively. Christian work is also the most effective method of winning lost souls for Christ.

However, this work wins but little applause from men, but it accomplishes great things for God. Jesus, the Master, is only one above the personal work. Among several advantages are the following fundamental ones:

A. All Can Do It.
Not everyone can preach, or prophesy, or teach in the congregation, but all can do the personal work. Even the one shut up at home by sickness can do personal work. As friends

come to the sick bed, a word of testimony can be given for Christ, or even an extended conversation can be held. In his book, 'How to work for Christ', R.A Torrey speaks of how a poor little girl in New York City, who was rescued from the slums and died a year or two afterwards, was used of God to lead about one hundred men and women to Christ, while lying upon her dying bed.

This shows us that even the servant girl can do effective personal work. Everyone can do personal work- the learned and the unlearned, a Sunday school child and a teacher; everyone can do. Every Pastor should urge this duty upon his people, train them for it, and see that they do it.

B. Personal work can be done anywhere

There is no one place where one cannot do personal work. We can do personal work on the street, whether street meetings are allowed or not. We can do personal work in the homes of the poor and in the homes of the rich, in hospitals, workhouses, jails, station houses, and all sorts of institutions - in a word, everywhere.

The Personal Work

C. Personal work can be done at any time

The times when we can have preaching services and Sunday schools are quite limited. As a rule, in most communities, we cannot have services more than two or three days in the week, and only three or four hours in the day, but personal work can be done seven days in the week, and any time of day or night. Sometimes personal work is best done at night, in the streets and public places.

I remember some time back around 1999 or 2000, one of our pastors used to evangelist to night callers while disguising himself as a Casanova. He won many night girls to Christ including the daughter of the famous king in Rumphi district. Those who love souls have walked the streets looking for wanderers, and have gone into dens of vice seeking the lost sheep, and hundreds upon hundreds of them have thus been found.

D. Personal Work Reaches All Classes.

There are large classes of men that no other method will reach. There are the shut-ins who cannot get out to church, the street-car men, the policemen, railroad conductors, sleeping-car men, firemen, the very poor and the very rich. As seen from biblical example, personal work can reach a brother (Jn.1:4-5), rulers (Jn.3:2, Acts 13:6-12), outcast (Lk.7:28), Christians (Acts 18:26-36), business men (Mt.4:18-22), travelers (Lk.20:30-37), Sinners (Lk.23:43, Jn.4:6-30), and all men (Acts 17:17).

F. Personal Work Hits the Mark

Preaching is necessarily general; personal work is direct and personal. There is no mistaking who is meant, there is no dodging the arrow, there is no possibility of giving away what is said to someone else. Many lost souls whom even expert Gospel preachers had missed have been reached by personal work afterwards.

G. Personal Work meets the definite need and every need of the person dealt with

Even when men are aroused and convicted, and perhaps converted, by a sermon, personal work is necessary to bring out into clear light and into a satisfactory experience one whom the sermon has thus aroused, convicted and converted.

H .Personal Work avails where other methods fail.

One of my best workers told me a few weeks

ago that she had attended church for years, and had wanted to become a Christian. She had listened to some of the best-known preachers, and still was unsaved, but the very first inquiry meeting she went into she was saved because someone came and dealt with her personally.

I. Personal Work produces very large results

There is no comparison whatever between what will be effected by good preaching and what will be affected by constant personal work. A church of many members, with the most powerful preaching possible, that depends upon the minister alone to win men to Christ by his preaching, would not accomplish anything like what would be accomplished by a church with a comparatively poor preacher, where the membership generally were personal workers.

3.
QUALIFICATIONS OF A CHRISTIAN WORKER

As previously said, Christian worker refers to a variety of Christians committed to do certain work whether at a local church level or on a wider range. This include parents, teachers, pastors, evangelists, missionaries, disciplers, Christian educators, youth and children workers, community evangelists, administrators, music directors, charity workers etc.

All of these have the same basic goals and principles that apply to their work. They may, indeed, differ in their daily activities and particular mean employed to them, but their core is the same – to accomplish the work of the Lord for the church. One consideration at the core of every kind of ministry is the quality of the person who is doing that ministry work. His character and attitude matters most than his talent or formal training.

A. A Personal Worker Must Be a Christian

By this I mean one must be genuine Christian, born again, grown up in many years of his life, and continuing to grow spiritually. Unless one is soundly converted, understands Christian experience, and all doctrine, he will not make a genuinely help to others. He must be able to know steps to salvation and has he gone through it.

How to Become a Christian

I am putting, here, some simple principles and steps to follow in order for one to become a Christian. The worker may use the same when leading sinner to repentance. If you have not gone through this yourself, please do so now in order to qualify for the kingdom and work of God.

   1. Realize that you are a sinner and hopelessly lost without God (Rom. 3:12, 23-24)

2. Believe the Good News that God sent forth His only begotten Son to take your place, and pay the full penalty for your sin (Rom.5:8) Today He is able to save you if you come to God through Him (Heb.7:25)

3. Confess with your mouth that you are a sinner, guilty before God and hopelessly lost (Rom.10:9-10). Remember, realizing, confessing, and repentance are three different things.

4. Accept the Lordship of Jesus Christ over your life (Rom.10:8-10). Renounce your old life and sin; invite Jesus to be the Lord and savior of your entire life.

5. Rely on God's promises, not upon your own feelings or theories (Rom.1:10)

6. Declare that you are saved by faith in the blood of Jesus Christ and His Gospel, and that you are forgiven by God, and are cleansed from all sin (Rom.3:24-25, Eph.2:8-9, 1 Jn.1:9).

B. A Personal Worker Must Live Right
Getting converted is but a first step, but how

The Personal Work

to live a Christian life is very important in the life of a man, especially a Christian worker.

How to live a Christian life

1 Believe the gospel and the entire word of God at all times of your life (1Jn.1:7)

2 Walk by faith, and not by sight, in the newness of your life (heb.10:23-29, Rom.6:1-23)

3 Read the Bible daily; search the scriptures, meditate on them and pray over it (Psa.1:1-2, 119:5, 2 Cor.10:4-7)

4 Pray daily to God as your heavenly father in the name of Jesus Christ, casting all your cares upon Him for cares for you (Phil.4:5-6, 1 Pet.5:7)

5 Claim all the benefits of the promises of God and appropriate by faith all that He has promised (Pet.1:1-4)

6 Keep your mind stayed upon God (Isa.26:3), and continue to grow in grace and in all virtues of grace (Phil.4:8, 1Pet.2:4-10)

7 Recognize at all times your weakness as well as God's strength and keeping power (1 Cor.10:12-13, 1Pet.1:5). Remember that faith is the victory that overcomes the world (1 Jn.5:1-4)

8 Confess the Lord Jesus frequently and daily as your personal savior and Lord (Mat.10:32-33)

9 Be busy at soul-winning and keep occupied in all phases of your Christian work possible (Pr. 11:30, Dan.12:3).

10 Avoid temptation and shun all evil companions (Ps.1, Pr.1:10-16, 1 Tim.4:6-16). Resist sin and Satan. Make friends with those of the faith and strive to be a blessing to them and other people (Rom.12:1 Cor.13, Col.3:10).

11 Attend church regularly (heb.10:25), co-operating with pastor and other leaders in all obedience and his labor (2 Cor.6:1, 2 Tim.2:15).

12 Seek God constantly for the anointing of the Holy Spirit, the fruit of the holy Spirit and gifts of the Holy Spirit,

and yield to, and obey the Holy Spirit guidance in all things (Lk.11:13; 24:49, Gal.5:16-26, Eph.5:18).

C. A Christian Worker Must Know the Bible

In whatever area of your work, the Bible is the greatest too. Therefore, every successful worker best knows his tool. A Christian worker must know his Bible from first book to the last one. He must know the basics such as the division of the Bible, the divisions of the books and location of the books. He must have a great deal of reference verses in order to carry out his work well. He must be able to accurately open the Bible.

D. Christian Worker Must Work In Love

Every other communication is contained in LOVE. God desires that work MUST come from a loving and willing heart (Jn.3:16, 1 Cor.13, 2 Cor.5:17-21, 1 Jn.3:1-11)

E. Christian Worker Must Have Faith in God's Work

One must always believe in what she or he is doing. He must have proper understanding of work he is doing. He must believe that from the impossible he can make the possible (Mt.17:20-21, Jn.10:10, 15:7, Heb. 11:6).

F. Christian Workers Must Use Wisdom
Christ is sending us as sheep among wolves most of which are found in the world. He challenges us to be as wise as a serpent and as honest as the dove (Mat.10:10). Serpents never unduly expose it to attacks, and the dove never provokes enmity. We have to ask God for wisdom, but we must ask in faith (Jas.1:5-6).

4.
ALL SHOULD WORK

A. Who should be a Christian Worker?
Honestly, God requires that every believer must work in the diversity of responsibilities. Every believer is gifted or talented to do a certain work. As earlier said, every believer is a member of the body of Christ; as such each member of the body has a designed purpose for the proper functioning of the body.

B. Why should all work?
1. God has commanded it in the Great Commission (Mt.28:19-20, Mk.16:15, Lk.24:47-50).

2. Al should work to show the genuineness of their faith and love for the Lord Jesus. Genuine love for our Lord can only be expressed in the keeping the commandments (Jn.15:10-14). Carrying on with the great commission is one of His commandments (Jas. 1:22-27, 2:14-26). Christian work is also an expression of love for others.

3. God chose and regenerated us for this purpose. "Ye have not chosen me, but I have chosen you, and ordained you, that ye should go and bring forth fruit, and that your fruit should remain: that whatsoever ye shall ask of the Father in my name, he may give it you" John 15:16. We are chosen so that we can bear fruits by winning souls for Christ.

4. Christ died that we might work. "Who gave himself for us, that he might redeem us from all iniquity, and purify unto himself a peculiar people, zealous of good works" Titus 2:14. The Holy Spirit sanctifies us within the parameters of the sacrifice of Christ so that we bring forth good works (2Cor.5:15-21).

The Personal Work

5. E Scriptures were given to qualify all believers for work. "All scripture is given by inspiration of God, and is profitable for doctrine, for reproof, for correction, for instruction in righteousness.; That the man of God may be perfect, thoroughly furnished unto all good works" 2 Tim 3:16-17. All we believe and teach must base on the infallible word of God – the scripture. Good understanding of scripture brings good word and proper works.

6. Sufficient help is given to all who work. "And God is able to make all grace abound toward you; that ye, always having all sufficiency in all things, may abound to every good work" 2 Cor. 9:8. God's grace and ability supply us with mental, physical and economical blessings for us to use for the good of others.

7. That we might partake in the blessings and rewards. As earlier indicated, there are rewards to be given to those who work successfully for God. "And they that be wise shall shine as the brightness of the firmament; and they that turn many to righteousness as the stars forever and ever" Dan 12:3. The wise are those who live for God and teach God's ways to others; those who make others wise and those who win souls and turn others to righteousness. They will have great reward. Can any wise Christian dare to ignore such a promise? God forbids.

8. That God might be glorified. "Let your light so shine before men, that they may see your good works, and glorify your Father which is in heaven" Matt 5:16. The purpose of all good works as believers is to glorify our heavenly Father (Jn.18:8, Tit.3:8).

9. That we might be pattern to others. Titus 2:7 "In all things showing thyself a pattern of good works: in doctrine showing incorruptness, gravity, sincerity." If Christ came to save Christian worker, then He came also to save the lost. Through our good works we demonstrate Christ to those we are working with (1 Tim.1:16).

10. Because we have a stewardship committed to us. 1 Cor. 4:1-2 "Let a man so account of us, as of the ministers of

Christ, and stewards of the mysteries of God. Moreover it is required in stewards that a man is found faithful." Usually, God does not demand success, rather He demands faithfulness. Good stewardship is being faithful to the work God has given us. Every believer is a steward in one way or the other (Lk.19:11-27)

11. Christian work is our privilege. Eph 3:8 "Unto me, who am less than the least of all saints, is this grace given, that I should preach among the Gentiles the unsearchable riches of Christ;".

12. It is every believer's Great Work. James 5:19-20 "Brethren, if any of you do err from the truth, and one convert him; Let him know, that he which converts the sinner from the error of his way shall save a soul from death, and shall hide a multitude of sins." It is the greatest w2ork to strengthen an individual, turning him back to the right way. It is saving a soul from death and hide multitude of sins of a sinner.

13. It pays well in joy and happiness. Matt 3:17-4:1 "And lo a voice from heaven, saying, 'This is my beloved Son, in whom I am well pleased." It brings joy and pleasure to us as well as to the heavenly Father to see that we have lived for Jesus, served Him faithfully, when most did the very opposite. We are considered the Lord's Jewels after serving Him faithfully (Mat.19:29).

14. Success is assured Beforehand: Isa 55:10-11 "For as the rain cometh down, and the snow from heaven, and returneth not thither, but watereth the earth, and maketh it bring forth and bud, that it may give seed to the sower, and bread to the eater: So shall my word be that goeth forth out of my mouth: it shall not return unto me void, but it shall accomplish that which I please, and it shall prosper in the thing whereto I sent it." God's word is not given just for a moment, but for the benefit of the people of all ages. No one can run away from doing the work knowing that success in imminent.

15. The World is Lost: 1 John 5:19 "And we know that we are of God, and the whole world lieth in wickedness." The whole world is embraced in the arms of

THE PERSONAL WORK

the devil, and is more or less asleep in death, transgression and sin (Eph.2:1-9). It is our responsibility as the redeemed to go out and save the lost by the power of the Holy Spirit.

5.
SOUL-WINNING

A. Terms used by Christian workers to define *soul-winning:*

1. ***Witnessing:*** "telling others about Christ" (I John 1:3).

2. ***Testifying:*** to speak of what you have personally experienced in your own life regarding salvation.

3. ***Personal outreach:*** "person-to-person dealing with men, women and children" that is, personally coming in contact with other persons, especially the unsaved.

4. ***Fishing for men:*** "going out into the ocean of sin and pulling drowning souls into the ark of safety" which is the Lord Jesus.

5. ***Personal evangelism:*** "telling of the Gospel to a sinner with the intent of bringing him to a saving knowledge of Christ." (Proverbs 11:30)

B. Soul-Winning is:

"The act of effectively convincing a lost person, through the use of God's Word and in the power of the Holy Spirit, of the facts:

1. That he is a sinner under the sentence of eternal death (John 3:36).
2. That Christ is the answer to his need (Acts 13:38, 39).
3. That the sinner must definitely accept Christ as Savior and Lord (John 12:48; II Thessalonians 1:8b).

It is the center of personal work. It is a mandate given to us by our Lord Jesus Christ (Mt. 28:19-23). The goal of this commission is to win souls for Christ. We may differ in the roles we play in the church, but the core of our work is the same –to win souls for

Christ, with an objective of Church growth –both local and universal church. Therefore, every Christian worker must do his work towards soul-winning.

C. Elements of Soul-winning

There are a lot of elements to be considered in soul-winning. Here, I have listed only ten most important principles which will be of a great help to every Christian worker. But, whenever and in whatever we do, we must bear in mind that we are not doing our garden work, but it is the garden of the Lord, the chief shepherd.

1. Tact: abilities to do and say the right thing at the right time and place

There is a need for ability to do and say the right thing at the right time and right place in soul-winning. The meeting of Jesus with the Samaritan woman serves as the right model for this in this regard (Jn.4:7-34). Notice how Jesus used tact in this conversation with the woman. See also John 8:1-11 and Acts 8:28-39.

2. Contact: Proper approach

Jesus began conversation with the Samaritan woman using the statement he knew the woman would respond to.

"Give me to drink" (Jn.4:7). He knew the bad relationship between the two tribes –Samaritans and the Jews, and the hatred therefore. He used the very ground to win the soul at this woman. Failure to approach will make us lose souls instead of winning them (Jn.8:1-11)

3. Knowledge: Clear understanding and application of data.
This refers mainly to clear understanding of the word of God, and how to apply them in a situation. Knowledge can be obtained through a thorough study of the word of God (2 Tim.2:15). The Christian worker must have the knowledge of the scriptures, believe its inspiration and power (2 Tim.3:15-17)

4. Faith: Absolute conviction regarding the word of God
We must believe with absolute conviction the creativity of the word of God. It is not just given for a moment, but for the benefit of achieving its purpose (Isa.55:10-11). It is impossible to please God without faith (Heb.11:6). We must work knowing that we have a Great Rewarder, who is our heavenly Father Jehovah God.

5. Love and Compassion: Devotion to Mercy for the lost souls

WE must feel pity and sympathy for the souls we are working on- those retarded children, orphans, widows, students, prisoners etc. They are fainted, and need a shepherd to care for them. You are that shepherd (Lk.19:10) Compassion is drawing and agitation of the innermost part at the sight of distressed or miserable people. It causes one to revolt to an action of deliverance for such misery and suffering.

6. Zeal: Eagerness to win lost souls

David had the zeal for the work in the house of the Lord. Likewise, our Lord Jesus Christ had the zeal to do the work of He who sent Him. We must not dare pleasing ourselves in all our work, but Him who called us. We must work to do the will of our Lord Jesus Christ (Psa.69:9, Jn.2:17).

7. Patience

In this case, patience refers to self-control, calmness, endurance, perseverance and forbearance. This is the fruit of the spirit in this life (Gal.5:22-23). This fruit can only be developing as we are led by the Holy Spirit. We can only be led by the Holy Spirit by making the cross the object of our faith.

8. Faithfulness

This is being true to duty, calling, vow or an obligation. It is said that if a believer is faithful with the little, He will likely be faithful in all other aspects of his Christian endeavors (Lk. 16:10-12, 1 Cor.4:1-2, 1 Pet.3:10-11). A Christian worker must be true to his task no matter how hard or small it is.

9. Appreciation

By this I mean being keenly aware and sensitive of the value of a lost soul. It must not be taken for granted as it is a valuable assert in the eyes of God. A Christian worker must know that one's soul is worth more than the whole world (Mk.8:36-38). We have to see the value in that one soul of a retarded child, or an elderly person, or a prisoner, unbeliever etc. Paul saw the value in the lives of the Gentiles and he was not discouraged by hostility of the Jews (Rom.9:1-2).

10. Responsibility

This is morally and legally obligated, and responsible for salvation of the lost souls. We must bear in mind that every person must have an opportunity to hearing the gospel. That is the responsibility of every Christian worker (Mk. 16:15). We must make sure that the saved person is grown to maturity, to the ultimate conclusion of total Christ-likeness (Phil.2:12-16).

6.
PRINCIPLES OF SOUL-WINNING

A. The Necessity of Evangelism

i. We are ambassadors of God on earth (2 Corinthians 5:20).

ii. Jesus gave us the Great Commission to preach the Gospel (Mark 16:15; Matthew 28:18-20; Luke 24:47; John 20:21).

iii. Jesus gave the Holy Spirit to empower us to preach the Gospel (Acts 1:8; Zech. 4:6; Acts 18:5).

iv. The Gospel of Christ is the only hope of salvation for sinners (Acts 4:12 cf. Romans 9:3; Matthew 9:36).

v. False religions and wrong ideas are capturing the minds and hearts of people (2 Corinthians 4:4).

B. The Message of Evangelism

i. Beware of preaching "easy-believism" as it is an oversimplified gospel.

ii. Be willing to spend time teaching the gospel and to wait for the Holy Spirit to produce genuine conviction of sin.

iii. Ensure that the following are found in the gospel message you present:

- It should be God -centered, not man-centered.
- It should fully represent Christ and His work of salvation.
- It should represent sin as an affront to God's Holiness.
- It should be bold to mention judgment and hell as the punishment for our sins.
- It should emphasize salvation through FAITH in Christ alone.
- It should clarify the cost of the Lordship of Christ.

The Personal Work

C. Communicating the Gospel

2 Tim. 3:16, 17 – "All scripture is given by inspiration of God, and is profitable for doctrine, for reproof, for correction, for instruction in righteousness: That the man of God may be perfect, thoroughly furnished unto all good works."

I. The Gospel is to be communicated personally:
- The main efforts of Jesus were put into building into the lives of a few people.
- Our goal is not to make converts, but to make disciples (Matthew 28:19).

II. The Gospel is to be communicated lovingly and gently
- Ephesians 4:15 – "speak the truth in love."
- 1 Peter 3:15 – "…be ready always to give an answer… with meekness and fear."
- Colossians 4:6 – "Let your speech be always with grace, seasoned with salt"

III. The Gospel is to be communicated comprehensibly
- Use simple words that are easy to

understand (cf. 1 Corinthians 9:20-23)

IV. The Gospel is to be communicated with the Use of Scripture

- Use God's Word wherever possible (Hebrews 4:12).
- It is not our clever speech or sound arguments that converts sinners but the Word of God which He promises will not return to Him void (Isaiah 55:11; cf. Acts 2:14-36).

V. The Gospel is to be communicated in Recognition of God's Sovereignty in Salvation:

- God is the One who calls a person irresistibly and effectually to salvation (John 6:44).
- Our part in evangelism is only twofold:

1. To present the complete gospel to him.
2. To pray that God will work in his heart (1 Tim. 2:1 4).

VI: Leave the Results to God:

- Don't think you have failed if you

The Personal Work

don't get results. (cf. Acts 17:32)
- Our responsibility is to sow the seed.
- Our success is measured by how well we have used the opportunities given to us to share the gospel with people around us.

7.
WHERE, WHEN & HOW

The mandate is to go in the utter most parts of the world. However, many Christians are ready to do the work, but they do not know where, when and how exactly they can do the work. Yes, we cannot all preach from the pulpit, but we can do the work from different areas and points.

Where to do Personal Work

A. Personal Work during the Gospel Meeting
The easiest and most natural place to do personal work is during Gospel meeting. Whenever you attend a meeting, watch for some-

one to deal with after the meeting is over. As the minister preaches the sermon keep your eyes on the audience and watch who it is that is hit and what hits them, then you can follow up the work that the minister has already done by his sermon. You must rather choose to play a role that will bring you closer to the audience in the gospel meeting- usher, deacon or anyone observing protocol in the audience. When it is well carried out it prevents any hopeful cases from getting out without being dealt with personally.

B. Visiting house-to-house

Gospel is best and successfully preached "from house to house" (Acts 20:20). There is far too little Christian work done in the home. The best home to begin with is your own Every man who is converted should begin to tell the saving power of Christ first in his own home, to his own relatives and friends (Luke 8:39. However, we should not limit our personal work to our own homes; we should do it in the homes where we visit. Thus, we should do personal work in the houses that we enter in our house-to-house visitation. The true visitor will find frequent opportunities for doing effective personal work with some of the inhabitants of the home, or with strangers they may find calling upon them.

C. On the Streets
Not only did the Apostle Paul reason "in the synagogue with the Jews and the devout persons," but also "in the market place every day with them that met with him." (Acts 17:17 R.V.) As you walk the streets, be listening for the voice of God to say "Go and speak to that man." Go out to the city or township streets with a mind of sharing the gospel to those God will direct you.

D. In the Hotels, parks and all places of Leisure
These places are often full of people who have plenty of leisure and are willing to talk upon almost any subject. Go through them and find your man, engage him in a conversation, and as quickly as you can, lead him up to the great subject that is burning in your own heart. Use the guides on how to do Christian work.

E. On a walk or ride
Jesus made the hearts of the two disciples burn within them while He spoke to them in the way, and opened to them the Scriptures

(Luke 24:32). Philip the evangelist was directed by the Holy Spirit to go and join himself to the chariot of Queen Candace's treasurer. The treasurer invited him up into the chariot to ride with him, and the memorable conversation and personal dealing that followed led to the conversion and baptism of the treasurer, and the carrying of the Gospel into Ethiopia (Acts 8:29-38).

F. At the places of business or work
And as he passed by, he saw Levi the son of Alpheus sitting at the receipt of custom, and said unto him, Follow me. And he arose and followed him. (Mark 2:14). This does not mean that we ought to interrupt men and hinder their proper performance of their business duties. As we do our usual businesses or work, there will, at least, rise an opportunity when we can have a chance just to drop a word or a little conversation with our mates. I remember having won to Christ two of my mates in a Wholesale shop I was working in 1996 using the same approach. They are now reliable church leaders in their various churches. There are five marks of a good opportunity; when one is alone, unoccupied, in good humor, communicative and in a serious mood.

G. In prisons, hospitals and other public institutions

A fine place to do personal work is in public institutions, such as prisons and hospitals, where many people are gathered together from morning till night. Every Sunday, all over this land, devoted men and women are going into prisons, jails and hospitals, carrying the glad tidings of salvation, and thousands are being converted to God through their faithful personal work.

Nurses in hospitals have a rare opportunity of doing personal work in the institutions where they are employed. My wife Laurent works in a government hospital at the maternity word; and she records a greatest number of women she has led to Christ through this method. R. A. Torrey observes that a very large proportion of trained nurses are devoted Christian women, and yet many of them do not realize the opportunities that God has put within their reach. Torrey observes further, "Indeed a true Christian physician will oftentimes find opportunities for doing personal work that even the minister of the Gospel cannot find. Sometimes it will be with the patient whom he is treating, sometimes with the relatives and friends of the patient who are in deep anxiety as to the outcome of the sickness."

When Should a Christian Work

Many may ask, "When should I begin to do Christian work?" Honestly, it should be "now", not "tomorrow". Jesus commands us to do the work of the Father 'now' while it is still a day (Jn.9:5). We should work whenever it is called 'today'. One has not to wait for an opportunity before he could do the work. He can start now; near-door, with the first neighbor to greet in the morning. God will hold all responsible for what is done in this matter (Ezek.3:18, 1 Cor. 3:11-15).

How to do Christian Work

One interesting thing about the Great Commission is that Jesus did not indicate how we should go about it. He only told us what He expects of us. Thus, Christian work can be done in many ways depending on the type of ministry one is carrying on with. However, since the essence of every ministry is to win souls for Christ, I will explain how soul winning can be done in this regard:

1. By personal evangelism with all the people's one comes into contact, and has

opportunity to speak to.
2. By giving out gospel tracts
3. By witnessing publicly
4. By house-to-house witnessing
5. By teaching and practicing the word of God
6. By all available other means which brings no shame to the name of the Lord.

There are certain steps to follow in doing soul winning:

A. The first thing is to find the one to deal with

When we go to church, or when we walk the street, when we are in the park, or on the train, or in a taxi, or in a bus, at the funeral ceremony, or at any public gathering, at the water hole, at school during break time, or the playground, or calling; in a word, whenever we have time that is not demanded by other duties we should look up to God and definitely ask Him to lead us to the one with whom we are to speak, if it is His will that we employ that time in work for Him. Further than this, we should be on the lookout for opportunities.

The Personal Work

B. Begin a conversation.

Having found your man, begin a conversation. Begin your conversation with few quick and leading questions like, Are you saved?" "Have you been born again?" "Upon what do you base your hope of eternal life?" "Are you confessing Christ openly before the world?" "Have you surrendered all you have and are to Christ?" Sometimes it is well to begin in this direct way even when you meet someone casually.

As a general rule, the question "Are you saved?" is a better one to ask than "Are you a Christian?" It sets one to thinking. However, there are many questions that can set the client thinking too. For example soul winner can ask, "Do you think that life is worth living?" You can also ask the client what he thinks in his opinion is the source of man's true happiness, or what he knows about of Christ and he personally knows him. Remember, knowing about someone is not the same thing as knowing him. Then continue from there.

C. Find out the client's stand

Having begun the conversation, find out as soon as possible where the person with whom you are dealing stands. By this I mean discover the class to which he belongs.

i. ***Ask him questions*** like, where do you stand, what do you believe?" Are you saved?" "Have you eternal life?" "Have you been born again?" "Do you know that you are a great sinner before God?" "Do you know that your sins are forgiven? "How he answers to these questions will determine your next step.

ii. ***Watch the inquirer's face***. A man's face will often reveal that which his words try to conceal. Anyone who cultivates a study of the faces of those with whom he deals will soon be able to tell in many instances their exact state irrespective of anything they may say.

iii. ***Observe his tone and manner.*** A man's tone or his manner often tells more than his words. A man who is not saved will very likely tell you that he is, but his tone and manner will reveal plainly that he is not. If one gets angry at you for asking these questions that reveals an uneasy conscience.

iv. ***Yield to the Holy Spirit***. If we look to Him to do it, He will often flash into our minds a view of the man's position, and just the Scripture that he needs.

D. Lead him as directly as you can to accept Jesus Christ as a personal Savior and Lord.

Use the "guides to become a Christian", to lead the client, as directly as we can, to accept Jesus Christ as a personal Savior and to surrender to Him as Lord and Master. We must always bear in mind that the primary purpose of our work is not to get people to join the church, or to give up their bad habits, but to help them to accept Jesus Christ as their Savior, and Lord. We have to point them to the cross.

8.
THE FOLLOW-UP

1. Introduction to follow-up ministry

A. The Goal of Follow-up:
- That God may be glorified
- As Christ is being formed in the life of the new Christian,
- Uniting him in the local body of believers
- And eventually reaching through him to others.

B. The Principles for Follow-up:
1. Specific prayer
2. The ministry of the Word of God
3. Individual attention

C. The Cost of Following up a New Christian:

1 It demands much time and commitment.

2 It demands much devoted effort to meet his needs in three areas:

- The principles and practice for his spiritual growth.
- The basic doctrines of the Christian faith.
- How to share Christ with his friends and neighbors.

D. How to tell if a new Christian is growing normally:

- He will become more like Jesus Christ (2 Corinthians 3:18).
- He will love others more (1 John 4:7).
- He will want to pray more (Galatians 4:6).
- He will want more of the Word of God (Acts 17:11, 1 Peter 2:2).

E. Biblical Examples of Follow-up

1. Paul, when he was converted (Acts 9:10-18)
2. New Christians at Antioch (Acts 13:38-44)

3. New Christians at Lystra, Iconium and Antioch (Acts 14:21-23)
4. Timothy (Acts 16:1-5)

2 The Process of Follow-up

A. Initial Follow-up
First, give an immediate follow-up advice when a person comes to Christ:
- How he can be sure of his salvation (Romans 8:16) Verses to use: John 3:36 and 5:24.
- That he should begin to talk about his faith. (Romans 10:10; Matthew 10:32)
- That he has only taken the first step in the life of discipleship.

B. Balanced Bible intake
The second step in the follow-up process is to arrange a place and time when you can meet again and have balanced Bible intake. Meet with the new Christian and go over the whole gospel once more.
- Begin your study with prayer.
- Read the notes, taking turns to read the paragraphs to each other.
- Stop at every Bible reference and ask him to find it in his Bible and read it aloud.

- When you come to questions, ask him what he thinks a possible answer might be.
- Keep each session fairly short (45 - 60 minutes). End with a short time of prayer.

C. Regular Quiet Time

The best way to show the new Christian what is meant by an effective quiet time is for you to go through one with him. Once he has started to have quiet times on his own, you can discuss them in your sessions with him. It may be useful for him to write down what he is learning in a notebook. Share with him what God has been showing you in your own quiet time.

3. Long-Term Follow-up - Various Methods

A. Find a new convert to follow-up

Follow-up through a Discipleship/cell group (2 Tim. 2:2)

- Advantage: It provides fellowship, love and care.
- Disadvantages: Conflicting personalities, different levels of motivation, and

varied abilities in the learning process.
- Effectiveness depends much on the leader of the group and his preparation for each study session.

B. How to conduct a study session

i. Introductory remarks and prayer (about 5 minutes).

ii. Most study outlines will be divided into 3 or 4 sections. Do the following for each section:

iii. Introduce it with a few remarks.
iv. Carefully guide the group through the section. All the verses quoted are to be looked up and read by different members.

v. Ask the right kind of questions - Open questions are best for stimulating discussion.

vi. Encourage those who are quiet to speak, and gently control those who are inclined to speak too long and too often.
vii. Briefly sum up the content of the section and any important considerations that have arisen during the discussion.

Then go to the next section.

viii. When all the sections are completed (30-40 minutes), make some concluding remarks and then have an open prayer session (10-15 minutes).

C. The use of books and tapes in follow-up:
1. Books: Choose books that cover the basics.
2. Cassette tapes: These are useful to follow-up busy people.

D. Follow-up by correspondence
This is useful when other methods are not possible.

4. Problems Encountered in Doing Follow-Up
The problems can best be dealt with patience, genuine love, wisdom. The most common problems are:

A. Unwillingness to meet you for follow-up
Possible causes:
- He is not converted at all.
- He may really be converted, yet peer pressure or home pressure is too strong for him, or some fears have gripped him.
- He does not relate to you personally.

- He does not understand why you should want to meet.

B. Unable to gain assurance of salvation.
Possible causes:
- He is not converted at all
- He has not told anyone what he now believes about Christ (cf. Rom. 10:9,10)

C. Afraid of identifying himself as a Christian.
If you are fairly assured that he is really converted you can:
- Remind him that Christ expects him to be a witness (Acts 1:8; 1 Pet 3:15; Rom 1:16)
- Encourage him to identify himself as Christian first to those who will appreciate him as such.
- Encourage him to pray to overcome his fear of letting others know he is a Christian.

D. Facing strong opposition from family and friends.
- Encourage him to show love to them.
- Tell him that he is bound to lose some of his closest friends because of his new

way of life. (Phil. 3:7, 8; Mt. 19:29; Ps. 1, Gal. 1:6-8; 1 Pet.4:12-14, Tit. 1:9.)

E. Not wanting to come to church.

- Take time to explain beforehand what goes on in church.
- Show clearly that coming to church is commanded by God (Heb. 1:24, 25) for God's glory, for our good and to edify others.

F. Wanting to have full victory over sin.

- Teach him that victory over sin is a lifelong process.
- Show him that he must depend on the Holy Spirit (Galatians 5:26-25)

9
Ministering To Backsliders

Today, Christians are surrounded There are two common groups of backsliders personal worker will frequently encounter with:

1. Careless Backsliders
These are those who make an open and avowed renouncing of Christ, men who have heart enmity against Christ and His cause. They are men, who in their minds approve their actions as right in renouncing Christ. They might have been discouraged while living as true Christians, so as to lead to their falling away. They are exactly the class of backslider being mentioned in Hebrews

THE PERSONAL WORK

6:4-6: "For it is impossible for those who were once enlightened, and have tasted of the heavenly gift, and were made partakers of the Holy Ghost; And have tasted the good word of God, and the powers of the world to come, If they shall fall away, to renew them again unto repentance; seeing they crucify to themselves the Son of God afresh, and put him to an open shame.

The impossible to renew them to repentance is not because the blood of Christ is not sufficient to obtain pardon for their sin; but that their sin, in its very nature, is opposite to repentance and everything that leads to it. Neither human wisdom nor knowledge would convince them to come back. It will require the great grace and fullness of the mercy of the Lord Jesus Christ to forgive them, even if they are not so willing to be forgiven. We have to approach such people with humble caution and prayers when dealing with them.

Passages to use on Careless Backsliders
There are a lot of passages we can use for winning back to the Lord a careless backslider I have ever used most of them, and it works. One or few of them can work to success. Never forget to remember that patience and humility pays in winning these backsliders.

Jeremiah 2:5: "Thus saith the Lord, What iniquity have your fathers found in me that they are gone far from me, and have walked after vanity, and are become vain?"

This same question must be driven home into their hearts; "What iniquity have you found in the Lord?" Dwell upon God's wonderful love to them, and show them the base ingratitude and folly of forsaking such a Savior and friend. Very likely they have wandered away because of the unkind treatment of some professed Christian, or of some minister, but hold them right to the point of how the Lord treated them, and how they are now treating Him.

Jeremiah 2:13: "For my people have committed two evils; they have forsaken me the fountain of living waters, and hewed them out cisterns, broken cisterns, that can hold no water."

Let the client make an affirmation of the verse. Humbly ask him questions such as, 'What does the Lord say that you forsook when you forsook Him?" "And to what does He say you turned?" "Is not that true in your experience? Did you not forsake the fountain of living waters, and have you not found the world broken cisterns that can hold no water? "Then illustrate the text by showing how foolish it would be to turn from a fountain of living water to broken cisterns or muddy pools.

Jeremiah 2:19: "Thine own wickedness shall correct thee, and thy backslidings shall reprove thee: know therefore and see that it is an evil thing and bitter, that thou hast forsaken the Lord thy God, and that my fear is not in thee, saith the Lord God of hosts."

1 Kings 11:9: "And the Lord was angry with Solomon, because his heart was turned from the Lord God of Israel, which had appeared unto him twice." Spice this with the story of a prodigal son found in Luke 15. Dwell on the details of verses 13-17.

Amos 4:11-12: "I have overthrown some of you, as God overthrew Sodom and Gomorrah, and ye were as a firebrand plucked out of the burning: yet have ye not returned unto me, saith the Lord. Therefore thus will I do unto thee, O Israel: and because I will do this unto thee, prepare to meet thy God, O Israel!"

Sometimes is better to have the client read the passage carefully and thereafter, ask him what the message of God to backsliding Israel was. Then ask him, "It is God's message to you too, as a backslider tonight, to 'prepare to meet thy God.'" Go over this again and again until the thought rings in the heart of the man.

2. Homesick Backsliders
These are those backsliders who are sick of their wandering and sin, and desire to come back to the Lord. They are a very different class from those just mentioned, though of course they are related. They are perhaps as easy a class to deal with as we ever find. There are many who once had knowledge of the Lord, but have wandered into sin, and who are now sick and tired of sin, and are longing to come back, but think that there is no acceptance for them.

Passages to use on homesick backsliders

Jeremiah 3:12-13, 22: "Go and proclaim these words toward the north, and say, Return, thou backsliding Israel, saith the Lord; and I will not cause mine anger to fall upon you: for I am merciful, saith the Lord, and I will not keep anger forever. Only acknowledge thine iniquity, that thou hast transgressed against the Lord thy God, and hast scattered thy ways to the strangers under every green tree, and ye have not obeyed my voice, saith the Lord. "Return, ye backsliding children, and I will heal your backslidings. Behold we come unto thee; for thou art the Lord our God."

This will show them how ready the Lord is to receive them back, and that all He asks of them is that they acknowledge their sin and return to Him.

Hosea 14:1-4 "O Israel, return unto the Lord thy God; for thou hast fallen by thine iniquity. Take with you words, and turn to the Lord: say unto him, Take away all iniquity, and receive us graciously: so will we render the calves of our lips. Asshur shall not save us; we will not ride upon horses: neither will we say any more to the work of our hands, ye are our gods: for in thee the fatherless findeth mercy. I will heal their backsliding, I will love them freely: for mine anger is turned away from him."

I concur with R.A Torrey (How to Work for Christ) that this passage is a tender invitation to penitent backsliders, and also shows the way back to God. He recalls having used this passage more frequently than almost any other with this class. Here, we see that God is inviting the backslider to Himself, and then, He promises to heal their backsliding and love them freely. All that God asks the backsliders is that they take words of confession and return to Him (verse 2).

Isaiah 43:22, 24-25: "But thou hast not called upon me, O Jacob; but thou hast been weary of me, O Israel...Thou hast bought me no sweet cane with money, neither hast thou filled me with the fat of thy sacrifices: but thou hast made me to serve with thy sins, thou hast wearied me with thine iniquities. I, even I, am he that blotteth out thy transgressions for mine own sake, and will not remember thy sins."

Isaiah 44:20-22: "He feedeth on ashes: a deceived heart hath turned him aside, that he cannot deliver his soul, nor say, 'Is there not a lie in my right hand?' Remember these, O Jacob and Israel; for thou art my servant: I have formed thee; thou art my servant: O Is-

The Personal Work

rael, thou shalt not be forgotten of me. I have blotted out, as a thick cloud, thy transgressions, and, as a cloud, thy sins: return unto me; for I have redeemed thee."

Jeremiah 29:11-13: "For I know the thoughts that I think toward you, saith the Lord, thoughts of peace, and not of evil, to give you an expected end. Then shall ye call upon me, and ye shall go and pray unto me, and I will hearken unto you. And ye shall seek me, and find me, when ye shall search for me with all your heart."

Deuteronomy 4:28,31: "And there ye shall serve gods, the work of men's hands, wood and stone, which neither see, nor hear, nor eat, nor smell...For the Lord thy God is a merciful God, He will not forsake thee, neither destroy thee, nor forget the covenant of thy fathers which he swore unto them."

2 Chronicles 7:14: "If my people, which are called by my name, shall humble themselves, and pray, and seek my face, and turn from their wicked ways, then will I hear from heaven, and will forgive their sin, and will heal their land."

1 John 2:1-2: "My little children, these things write I unto you, that ye sin not. And if any man sin, we have an advocate with the Father, Jesus Christ the righteous, and he is the propitiation of our sins: and not for ours only, but also for the sins of the whole world."

10.
ANSWERING DOUBTS AND EXCUSES

1. "I am afraid of parental persecution if I become a Christian."
- There are many things in life he has to decide for himself (e.g. marriage)
- We are all accountable before God individually (Rom 14:12)
- He should put God first and seek Him (2 Tim 2: 12, Acts 5:29)

2. "There are so many professing Christians who are hypocrites. I don't want to be like them."
- His faulty reasoning - Just because

we have tasted a rotten apple, does it mean that all apples are bad.
- The important thing is to be sincere about what we believe and to seek God with all our hearts.

3. "How do I know that there is a God?"

A. The arguments or rational proofs for the existence of God:
- The cosmological argument   argument from the existence of the world
- The teleological argument   argument from purpose (or end/telos)
- The anthropological argument   argument from man
- The moral argument   argument from morality (i.e. right & wrong)

B. Tell him that there is only one God (monotheism) and not many gods (polytheism) (Isa. 45:14,18, 21:22). Isa 44:6 "Thus saith the LORD the King of Israel, and his redeemer the LORD of hosts; I am the first, and I am the last; and beside me there is no God."

4. "Why should I accept the Bible as the final authority from God? Why not the Koran or Buddhist scriptures or the

Apocrypha? They are equally good."

- The Bible is verbally & planarity inspired of God (2 Tim 3:16,17; 1 Pet 1:19 21)
- It is God's special revelation to man, with no mistakes and whatever it said is true and authoritative.
- It is authenticated by history and archaeology and has been miraculously preserved all these centuries.

5. "I am neutral in religion. I believe all religions are good and all of them will lead us to heaven."

- Jesus is the only way to God (John 14:6; Acts 4:12)
- While all religions may have some good morality, this is not the same as salvation.
- Christianity is about a relationship with God and knowing Him in a personal way through Christ. (John 17:3)
- We are either for Christ or we are not. (Mat 12:30)

6. "If there is a God, why does He allow evil in this world?"

- God created all things according to His perfect will, but that He also gave

men the responsibility to choose. (Eccl 7:29)
- When man chose to disobey God, sin and its consequences brought about our present circumstances with both moral and physical evil (Gen 3:16-19).
- Only God Himself can save us and deliver us from a world that is evil and destined for destruction. (Gal 1:3,4)
- God has a purpose for allowing moral and physical evil to exist. (Rom 8:28)
- God will one day triumph over evil and punish all those who oppose Him. (Eph 5:5,6)

7. "I am too busy with my world. After I established my business, I will consider Christ one day!"
- This is short-sighted and disastrous (Mark 8:36; Luke 12: 20).
- There is not as much time as he thinks. (2 Cor. 6:2; Psa. 90:10; Jas 4:14).
- By the time his 'one day' comes it may be too late (Isa 55:6; Heb. 12:17).

8. "I cannot understand everything about the Bible."
- We make use of many things we do not fully understand. We do not under-

stand everything about medicine or electricity, and yet we use them.

9. "There is too much to give up."

- Nothing is more important than his soul. (Mk 8:36)
- God loves sinners enough to give up His Son. (Rom 8:32; Jn. 3:16)
- The things he loves in this world will pass away. (1 Jn. 2:15 17)
- What he gets as a believer will exceed all that he gives up. (Lk 18:29 30)

10. "I am too great a sinner."

- Jesus came into the world to save sinners. (Mt 9:12 13; Lk 19:10)
- Paul was the chief of sinners, and yet he could be saved. (I Tim 1:15)
- Jesus turns no one away. (Jn. 6:37)

11. "I must become better before I can believe in Christ."

- We go to the doctor when we fall sick. We do not wait to get better before seeing the doctor. (Mt 9:12 13; Lk 18:13 14)
- He can never become better before he receives Christ (Eph 2:1-4)

12. "I need to see a sign before I can believe."

- It is wrong to seek for signs. (Mt 12:38 39)
- If he cannot believe the Bible he will not believe at all miracle or no miracle. (Lk 16:27 31)
- God has already given us many signs in Creation (Rom 1:20), in Science (Job 26:7), and in Prophecy: (Deut. 30:3)

13. "I can make it to heaven by my good works."

- In order to be saved by good works we must keep all the laws of God without breaking any one of them. The breaking of just one law will render us guilty. (Gal 3:10 1 1; Jas 2:10)
- In reality good works cannot wash away our sins. (Jn. 8:24)
- Nobody in the world can do good perfectly. (Eccl 7:20; Rom 7:19 24)
- No man can be saved by depending on his own good works (Isa 64:6).

14. "How about those who have never heard of Christ?"

- These people are not innocent. (Rom 3:10; Rom 3:23)

The Personal Work

- God's laws are already written in their hearts. (Rom 2:14 15; Rom 1:32)
- God is righteous in judgment. (Deut. 32:4; Gen 18:25)

15. "What about the beliefs of rebirth, nirvana, etc.?"

- The end result of rebirth and reincarnation is to pay for all our sins or to have a zero account with regards to our sins. But in the first place, when we first entered into the world, we have to be logically "sinless" because we have not committed any sins yet.
- Why an all-powerful would and all-knowing God require so many births and rebirths to know who we are? God, because of His foreknowledge, knows who we are or what we will be like even before we are actually born.
- Life's suffering is not the results of bad past karma but rather in accordance to the foreknowledge and purpose of God. Some people are born blind, deaf or retarded, not because of some bad, past karma but because God may use such handicaps to help these people come to know Him.
- The Bible teaches eternal judg-

ment rather than rebirth ((Lk.16:22 24; Heb.3:27)

11.
Dealing with Skeptics and Infidels

First, the worker must know the different types of the skeptics and infidels, and how to best deal with each group type.

1. Mere Triflers Skeptics
This is the largest group of skeptics in our day. They only profess being skeptic as an excuse for sin, and a relief for their own consciences. Never spend much time with such, but just give them something that will convict their conscience. A good passage for this purpose is 1 Corinthians 1:18. This is the very thing skeptic says- the Bible and the Gospel is foolishness to them. The Bible agrees with

them, so do us.

"For the preaching of the cross is to them that perish foolishness; but unto us which are saved it is the power of God." 1 Cor.1:18.

Other passages for this purpose include 1 Cor. 2:14, 2 Thess. 1:7-9, John 3:36, 2 Thess. 2:10-12, Ps. 14:1

2. Earnest-Minded Skeptics

These are those who are very desirous of knowing the truth, but who are in an utter confusion of skepticism. This is the most interesting group to work with. In beginning work with them, it is well to ask them the following preliminary questions:

A. "What Can't You Believe?"

Get as full an answer as possible to this question, for many a man thinks he is a skeptic when really he does believe the great fundamental truths. This will also give a worker a starting point.

B. "Why Can't You Believe?"

This will oftentimes show the man how utterly without foundation is his grounds for unbelief.

C. "Do You Live Up To What You Do Believe?"

This will give you an opportunity in many cases to show a man that his trouble is not so much what he does not believe, as his failure to live up to what he does believe.

D. What Do You Believe?"

A few important lines along which to carry out this inquiry are, "Do you believe that there is an absolute difference between right and wrong?" "Do you believe that there is a God?" "Do you believe in prayer?" "Do you believe any part of the Bible, if so what part? "Then proceed by showing him how to believe through the following passages: John 7:17; 20:31: and many more especially from the book of John which shows that Christ is the Son of or God.

3. Special Classes of Skeptics

There are several subclasses of this special class of skeptics and infidels. Most of these include Humanists, atheists and many others.

A. Those Who Doubt the Existence of God

In addition to the fact that we can use those passages given in the previous classes, there are also some excellent passages to be specially used for this class. The most excellent passages include:

Rom. 1:19-22: "Because that which may be known of God is manifest in them; for God hath shewed it unto them. For the invisible things of him from the creation of the world are clearly seen, being understood by the things that are made, even his eternal power and Godhead; so that they are without excuse: Because that, when they knew God, they glorified him not as God, neither were thankful; but became vain in their imaginations, and their foolish heart was darkened. Professing themselves to be wise, they became fools"

Ps 19:1-4: "The heavens declare the glory of God; and the firmament sheweth his handiwork. Day unto day uttereth speech, and night unto night sheweth knowledge. There is no speech nor language, where their voice is not heard. Their line is gone out through all the earth, and their words to the end of the world. In them hath he set a tabernacle for the sun."

Ps 14:1: "The fool hath said in his heart, 'there is no God. They are corrupt, they have done abominable works, there is none that doeth good." Denying the existence of God is being foolish; and it leads to eternal damnation.

B. Those Who Doubt That the Bible Is the Word of God

I have ever come across men who say that they do not believe the whole Bible is the Word of God, but that it contains the word of God, and also that the Old Testament is not part of Jesus' authority. There are also many Christian churches that believe the same lie. Most of them do not accept the authority of the Old Testament. But if one accepts the authority of Jesus, he must also accept the authority of the Old Testament because Jesus ascribed authority to it; He quote from it.

Here are the passages to use on such:

John 10:35: "If he called them gods, unto whom the word of God came, and the scripture cannot be broken." Jesus quotes from Psalm 82:6.

Luke 24:27, 44: "And beginning at Moses and all the prophets, he expounded unto them in all the scriptures the things concerning himself. And he said unto them, 'These are the words which I spake unto you, while I was yet with you, that all things must be fulfilled, which were written in the law of Moses, and in the prophets, and in the psalms, concerning me.'"

Jesus quoted the entire Old Testament Scriptures, Moses and the prophets, as being of conclusive authority. He set the stamp of His authority upon the whole Old Testament. Therefore, if one accepts the authority of Christ, he must accept the authority of the whole Old Testament.

1 Thess. 2:13: "For this cause also thank we God without ceasing, because, when ye received the word of God which ye heard of us, you received it not as the word of men, but as it is in truth, the word of God, which effectually worketh also in you that believe."

2 Peter 1:21: "For the prophecy came not in old time by the will of man: but holy men of God spake as they were moved by the Holy Ghost."

Rom 3:3-4: "For what if some did not believe? Shall their unbelief make the faith of

The Personal Work

God without effect? God forbid: yea, let God be true, but every man a liar; as it is written, that thou mightiest be justified in thy sayings, and mightiest overcome when thou art judged."

12.
Muhammad, Islam & Qur'an

1. Brief Overview
A. What is Islam?
Islam is the world's youngest major world religion. It claims to be the restoration of original monotheism and truth and thus supersedes both Judaism and Christianity. It stresses submission to Allah, the Arabic name for God, and conformity to the "five pillars" or disciplines of that religion as essential for salvation.

From its inception, Islam was an aggressively missionary-oriented religion. Within one century of its formation, often using military force, Islam had spread across the Middle East, most of North Africa, and as far east as

India. While God is, in the understanding of most Muslims, unknowable personally, His will is believed to be perfectly revealed in the holy book, the Qur'an. The Qur'an is to be followed completely and its teachings form a complete guide for life and society.

Today, Islam has a worldwide estimated membership of 1.28 billion; 69 percent live in South and Southeast Asia; 27 percent in Africa; 4 percent other; United States: Estimated 5 to 8 million. It has left no country in Africa. North Africa and some parts on northwest parts have become the homes of Islam. There is almost equal share of Islam and Christianity in the eastern parts of Africa.

B. Who Was Muhammad?

Muhammad is believed by Muslims to be the last and greatest prophet of God-"the seal of the prophets." It was through him that the Qur'an was dictated, thus according him the supreme place among the seers of God. A native of Mecca, Muhammad was forced to flee that city in A.D. 622 after preaching vigorously against the paganism of the city. Having secured his leadership in Medina, and with several military victories to his credit,

Muhammad returned in triumph to Mecca in A.D. 630. There, he established Islam as the religion of all Arabia.

C. What Is the Qur'an?

The Qur'an is the sacred book of Islam and the perfect word of God for the Muslim. It is claimed that the Qur'an was dictated in Arabic by the angel Gabriel to Muhammad and were God's precise words. As such, it had preexisted from eternity in heaven with God as the "Mother of the Book" and was in that form uncreated and coeternal with God. Islam teaches that it contains the total and perfect revelation and will of God.

The Qur'an is about four-fifths the length of the New Testament and is divided into 114 "surahs" or chapters. While Islam respects the Torah, the psalms of David and the four Gospels, the Qur'an stands alone in its authority and absoluteness. It is believed to be most perfectly understood in Arabic and it is a religious obligation to seek to read and quote it in the original language.

2 What Are the Five Pillars of Islam?

They are the framework for the Muslim's life

The Personal Work

and discipline. Successful and satisfactory adherence to the pillars satisfies the will of Allah. They form the basis for the Muslim's hope for salvation along with faith and belief in Allah's existence, the authority of Muhammad as a prophet, and the finality and perfection of the Qur'an.

D. The five pillars are:

1. The Confession of Faith or Shahada: It is the declaration that there is no god but Allah and Muhammad is his prophet. Sincerity in the voicing of the confession is necessary for it to be valid. It must be held until death and repudiation of the Shahada nullifies hope for salvation.

2. Prayer or Salat: Five times a day, preceded by ceremonial washing, the Muslim is required to pray facing Mecca. Specific formulas, recited from the Qur'an (in Arabic), along with prostrations are included. Prayer is, in this sense, an expression of submission to the will of Allah. While most of Islam has no hierarchical priesthood, prayers are led in mosques by respected lay leaders. The five times of prayer are before sunrise, noon, mid-afternoon, sunset, and prior to sleep.

3. Almsgiving or Zakat: The Qur'an teaches the giving of two and one-half percent of one's capital wealth to the poor and/or for the propagation of Islam. By doing so, the Muslims' remaining wealth is purified.

4. The Fast or Sawm: During the course of the lunar month of Ramadan, a fast is to be observed by every Muslim from sunrise to sunset. Nothing is to pass over the lips during this time, and they should refrain from sexual relations. After sunset, feasting and other celebrations often occur. The daylight hours are set aside for self-purification. The month is used to remember the giving of the Qur'an to Muhammad.

5. Pilgrimage or Hajj: All Muslims who are economically and physically able are required to journey as a pilgrim to Mecca at least once in their lifetime. The pilgrim's required simple dress stresses the notion of equality before God. Another element of the Hajj is the mandatory walk of each pilgrim seven times around the Kaabah-the shrine of the black rock, the holiest site of Islam. Muhammad taught that the Kaabah was the original place of worship for Adam and later for Abraham. The Kaabah is thus venerated as the site of true religion, the absolute monotheism of Islam.

E. The Doctrines of Islam

God: He is numerically and absolutely one. God is beyond the understanding of man so that only His will may be revealed and known. He is confessed as the "merciful and compassionate one."

Sin: The most serious sin that can be ascribed to people is that of "shirk" or considering God as more than one. Original sin is viewed as a "lapse" by Adam. The fallen nature of humankind is not endorsed by Islam. Humankind is considered weak and forgetful but not as fallen.

Angels: Islam affirms the reality of angels as messengers and agents of God. Evil spirits or Jinn also exist. Satan is a fallen angel. Angels perform important functions for God both now and at the end of time.

Final Judgment: The world will be judged at the end of time by God. The good deeds and obedience of all people to the five pillars and the Qur'an will serve as the basis of judgment.

Salvation: It is determined by faith, as defined by Islam, as well as by compiling good deeds primarily in conformity to the five pillars.

Marriage: Muslims uphold marriage as honorable and condemn adultery. While many Muslim marriages are monogamous, Islamic states allow as many as four wives. Men consider a woman as less than an equal, and while a man has the right to divorce his wife, the wife has no similar power (see Surah 2:228; 4:34). Nonetheless, the female has a right to own and dispose of property. Modesty in dress is encouraged for both men and women.

War: The term jihad or "struggle" is often considered as both external and internal, both a physical and spiritual struggle. The enemies of Islam or "idolaters," states the Qur'an, may be slain "wherever you find them" (Surah 9:5.) (See Surah 47:4.) Paradise is promised for those who die fighting in the cause of Islam (see Surah 3:195; 2:244). Moderate Muslims emphasize the spiritual dimension of jihad and not its political element.

Diet and Food: Muslim dietary codes forbid the eating of pork and the use of intoxicating drinks. Other meats may be eaten from animals slaughtered by devout Muslims. Healthy diet and lifestyle are encouraged.

13.
EVANGELIZING THE MUSLIM BROTHER

1. Muslim Objections to Christianity

Christians and Jews are acknowledged as "people of the book," although their failure to conform to the confession of Islam labels them as unbelievers. Following are several questions that Muslims have about Christianity.

A. Is the Trinity a belief in three gods?

Christians are monotheistic and believe that God is one. But both in His work in accomplishing salvation through the Person of Jesus Christ and through biblical study it has become clear that His oneness in fact comprises three Persons- Father, Son (Jesus Christ), and the third Person of the Godhead, the Holy Spirit. Mary is not part of the Godhead. The notion of God, who is three-in-one, is part of both the mystery and greatness of God. God is in essence one while in Persons three. This truth helps us understand God as truly personal and having the capacity to relate to other persons. As well, Christians confirm the holiness, sovereignty, and greatness of God.

B. How can Jesus be the Son of God?

Scripture affirms that Jesus was conceived supernaturally by the Holy Spirit and was born of the Virgin Mary. It does not in any way claim that Jesus was directly God the Father's biological and physical son. It rejects the notion of the Arabic word for son walad, meaning physical son, for the word ibin, which is the title of relationship. Jesus is the Son in a symbolic manner designating that He was God the Word who became man in order to save humankind from its sin. The virgin birth was supernatural as God the Holy Spirit conceived in Mary, without physical relations, Jesus the Messiah. In this manner even the Qur'an affirms the miraculous birth of Christ (see Surah 19:16-21). Jesus was in this sense "God's unique Son." During His earthly ministry He carried out the will of the Father. Notably the Qur'an affirms Jesus' supernatural birth, life of miracles, His compassion, and ascension to heaven. (see Surah 19:16-21,29-31; 3:37-47, 5:110.)

C. How could Jesus have died on the cross, especially if He's God's Son?

The testimony of history and of the Injil or the four Gospels is that Jesus died on the cross. If it is understood that God is love, and that humankind is lost in sin, then is it not likely that God would have provided a sacrifice for sin? Jesus is God's sacrifice for all the sins of the world and is a bridge from a holy God to fallen and sinful humans.

This truth is revealed in the Injil-John 3:16. Even the Qur'an states in Surah 3:55 that "Allah said: O Isa [Jesus], I am going to terminate [to put to death] the period of your stay (on earth) and cause you to ascend unto Me."[1] What other way could this concept have any meaning apart from Jesus' death for sin and His subsequent resurrection?

Muslims believe that God took Jesus from the cross and substituted Judas in His place, or at least someone who looked like Jesus. He was then taken to heaven where He is alive and from where one day He will return.

2. Answering Muslims' Questions to Christians about Islam

A. *What do you think about the prophet Muhammad?*

Muhammad was apparently a well-meaning man who sought to oppose paganism and evil in his day. While he succeeded in uniting the Arabian Peninsula and upheld several important virtues, we do not believe he received a fresh revelation from God. Jesus Christ fulfilled not only the final prophetic role from God, but He is the Savior of the world and God the Son. While Islam believes that some Bible passages refer to Muhammad (see Deut. 18:18-19; John 14:16; 15:26; 16:7), that is clearly not the meaning of the texts. Other passages may help in understanding and interpreting the previous texts (see Matthew 21:11; Luke 24:19; John 6:14; 7:40; Acts 1:8-16; 7:37).

B. What is your opinion of the Qur'an?
It is a greatly valued book for the Muslim. It is not received or believed to be a divine book by the Christian. The statements of the Qur'an are accepted only where they agree with the Bible.

C. What is your opinion about the five pillars?
Salvation is from God and comes only through the saving work of Jesus Christ. When we put our faith in Him, we will be saved (see John 3:16-21,31-36).

3. Witnessing to Muslims
As you evangelize to the Muslim brother, the Christian worker must remember to bear in mind and apply certain principles

1. Stress that because of Jesus, His cross, and resurrection, one may have the full assurance of salvation, both now and for eternity (see 1 John 5:13). Share the plan of salvation with the Muslim. Point out that salvation is a gift and not to be earned.

2 Pray for the fullness of the Holy Spirit. Trust Him to provide wisdom and grace.

The Personal Work

3 Be courteous and loving. Be willing to become a friend and a personal evangelist to Muslims. Treat Muslims as objects of concern, not notches in your belt!

4 Do not soft-pedal around biblical terminology to please Muslim hearers. Be clear about what you believe and why you believe it. Know the Scriptures well, and know the confessions and what exactly you believe (catechisms). The more you know about your faith, the easier it is to talk with Muslims. The testimony of the Gospels provides the most reliable witness to Christ. Preach the Gospel as it is!

5. Reflect interest in their beliefs. Allow them time to articulate their views. Be acquainted with their basic beliefs and be willing to examine passages of the Qur'an concerning their beliefs.

6. Our goal is to open up their minds a bit so that they can start reading the Gospels for an eyewitness or a companion of an eyewitness to the real Jesus . There is no gospel in Islam. While claiming to be the perpetual religion of nature and history, following in the footsteps of Christianity, it attempts to justify its claims by asserting that the Word of God, revealed in the New and Old Testament, is corrupted. Our apologetic discussion with Muslims should be to defend the Scriptures and prove that the Scriptures aren't corrupt as Muslims claim.

7. Always ask them the classic evangelistic questions. 'What about your salvation?' 'Can you be certain of this?' 'If you were to die, can you be certain you'd enter heaven at some point?' Their response is always, "No, I couldn't be certain, nor do I care."

8. The essence of Muslim evangelism is accurate communication about sin and grace: simply and clearly. Talk about the law and the gospel, not about infralapsarianism and divine simplicity! Don't compare the Bible with the Quran. That comes later.

9 Always remember that you are talking to Muslims. Avoid the use of Christian jargon. Speak about real sin, real guilt, and real shed blood! Do not be ashamed to use Jesus' direct and indirect titles clearly such as 'Son of God' 'Lamb of God' 'New Adam' 'I AM - YAHWEH' 'Savior' 'Almighty God'

THE PERSONAL WORK

10. Be sensitive to their past - if they've had a bad experience with Christians, missionaries or churches, struggled with a particular sin etc., be understanding and compassionate! Muslims hate self-righteousness, and rightly so! Do not soft-pedal the law and the guilt of sin, but make sure they understand that you are a justified sinner, not a self-righteous "know it all" who is here to correct them!

11. Don't feel like you have to answer all of the questions Muslim will ask you regarding your faith in one day. However, make sure they hear your answers to one or two questions clearly. Stick with the subject - don't get sidetracked. When the conversation wanders, pull it back to center stage - the law and the gospel

12. It is okay to offend the Muslims by being very clear about the teachings of Christ! They will not convert to Christ if they are not offended by the message of the Gospel. The message of the Gospel offends Muslims. It is okay! Don't worry! God will take care of the hearer. It is His message.

13. Do not use any 'Muslim friendly' bible translations. 'Muslims friendly' bible translations are very deceptive! They are not true to the original Scriptures. Muslims see it as a form of deception by missionaries.

14. The aim of Evangelism to Muslims is not to win an argument, but to lead Muslims to Christ. Discussions may get heated and intense at times - that's okay. But the purpose of Muslim evangelism is not to show why you are right and Islam is wrong. It is to communicate the truth of the gospel! The message is to be the offence! Not you!

15. Use tact and wisdom. When Muslims are apathetic about sin - use the law. When Muslims have doubts or are skeptical - use basic apologetic arguments. When Muslims express guilt for sin - present the Gospel.

16. When talking to Muslims stick with what all Christians hold in common wherever possible. Leave the internecine fighting among Christians aside when talking to Muslims. A Muslim will not care so much about differences between the Catholics and the Protestants or Lutherans and Baptists. Issues such as the exact meaning of the Lord's Supper or methods of baptism should be addressed later, during discipleship!

The Personal Work

17. Wherever possible, when talking to Muslims speak about Christianity as factually true - "Jesus did this," "Jesus said this," "people heard and saw him," etc. Keep away from the subjective line of approach-- "it works for me," "this is how I feel about it," this is my testimony."

18. Trust in the power of God the Holy Spirit working through the word. Muslims will respect the text you quote, but not your personal opinion. Cite texts directly from the Scriptures with attribution. Jesus says, Paul says.... It will not help Muslims to hear your personal opinion on biblical issues. So, don't say "I think," or "it seems to me" or "I feel like…" Muslims interpret your thoughts, your take on things or your feelings as part of the corruption of the Bible

19. Don't rush things with Muslims. Just because a Muslim is not ready to trust in Christ after one encounter does not mean that effective evangelism has not taken place. Pre-evangelism is equally vital. You may plant, but someone else may have to water! Always remember that it is not us who convert the Muslims to Christ but God Himself (in His time)!

20. Remember that evangelism isn't complete after you first present the Gospel message to a Muslim. Evangelism has to continue even after they repent and give their lives to Christ. They have to sit under the ministry of the Word. Evangelism of a Muslim is complete only after they are baptized, brought to the Lord's Supper and sat under the preaching of the Word at church. In other words, evangelism never ends. Discipleship is evangelism.

21. Don't force things. If your Muslim friends balk, ridicule and otherwise are not interested, back off. Find another time and place. If after repeated attempts to communicate the gospel, and someone still shows an unwillingness to hear what you have to say, "shake the dust off your feet and move on to a new town!"

22. Be willing to get your Muslim friends the resources they need: be willing to provide them with a Bible (not just a New Testament), the right book to read, and certainly an invitation to your home and later an invitation to attend your church or to a Bible study, etc. Never ever use a Muslim friendly bible translation. These translations are a product of some western mission agencies without any support from the national churches who know their context best.,

23. Show your Muslim friends some samples of Christian biblical songs with verses directly taken from Scriptures. In other words, sing the Bible to them! The role of music in human culture is to join people together. Biblically we are commanded to sing the praises of Christ. There are 694 references to singing or music making in Holy Scriptures. Participatory singing is a very significant matter biblically. There will be no singing in Hell, but the saints in Heaven will sing everlastingly. That is really amazing and remarkable! Let us show Muslims what we will be doing in Heaven.

14.
DEALING WITH JEHOVAH'S WITNESSES

The theological points held by the Jehovah's Witnesses differ much from orthodox Christianity. Among many objections by the JWs are their denial of the deity and divinity of Jesus Christ, denial of the Holy Trinity, and of the eternal punishment.

1. Some recent Common Doctrine of the JWS (1997 edition)

1. Jesus is not God. He was originally created by God as the Archangel Michael who later became man.

2. Holy Spirit is not a personality, but

God's force

3. Heaven is the home of God. Majority of believers will not spend eternity with God there for they inherit the earth.

4. Believers will not immediately be with Christ after death. They remain in a soul sleep until his second coming.

5. There is no eternal punishment since God cannot torture us, but the sinners will be inhaled.

2. JWs' Approach

JW's are very sincere, caring, and better students of the Bible. Therefore, extra caution is needed when talking with them. They will first tell you what is in agreement with the beliefs of most Christians. However, their beliefs begin to differ from those of orthodox Christians when they mention that Christ is going to permanently reign on a refurbished Earth, not in heaven. They also teach that Jesus was created by God and is inferior to God.

JW's believe in Bible's preservation and inspiration by God. However, the difference is on their translation and interpretation of other verses. Therefore, they prefer their NWT to suit their interpretations which they claim is much more accurate than other English translations. However, there is no consensus of scholarship that has recommended this translation.

When talking to JW's it is easy to get sidetracked and move from one issue to another. So, be careful and stick to one important issue of all; the deity of Jesus Christ. Jehovah's Witnesses do not believe in the deity of Jesus Christ. This will keep the conversation on the focal point that separates JW's from Christians.

When you begin talking with them, limit your conversation to the question, **"Who is Jesus?"** This is the most important difference between their beliefs and historical Christianity. Tell them you would like to hear their reasons for believing Jesus is a creation of God, and then you would like their responses to your reasons for believing he is God. Then dialogue with them.

Tell them that they have not provided any good reasons for believing Jesus was created and that you have provided five reasons why he is God, one which even exposes some inconsistencies in their own translation of the

Bible. JW's may try to answer arguments for the deity that you never raised. This can create an illusion that you stand corrected on the deity issue. Insist that you stay on the issue of who Jesus is, because its importance is far greater than whether eternity is spent in heaven or on a heavenly earth ruled by Christ

3. Answering the Jehovah Witnesses

Jehovah's Witnesses have six main texts they use against the deity of Jesus Chris. They use New World Translation to their advantage when interpreting the scriptures.

I. Revelation 3:14: "And to the angel of the congregation in Laodicea write: These are the things that the Amen says, the faithful and true witness, *the beginning of the creation by God."* NWT

JW Interpretation: "the beginning of the creation by God" means Jesus was the first thing created by God.

Refutation: The Greek word for 'beginning' is 'arche' used in different shades of meaning throughout the Bible.

    A. Time: When a word is used in the active sense, it is producing the action;

in other words, Jesus was the "beginning one" or the originating source of creation (i.e., the Creator).

B. Political: When arche is used in this manner it means a government or ruler (Luke 20:20). Arche is the top (or beginning) of a power hierarchy (the president is arche of the government). Thus, If John means arche in a political sense, the verse may be translated "the ruler of God's creation" (NIV).

In order to translate and interpret a verse correctly, there are four general rules that can be helpful:

1. Consider the various meanings of a word as discussed above.

2. Consider the verse and see if any particular meaning fits best The NWT renders this verse in such a manner that Jesus was the first thing created "by God" which does not appear in Greek texts.

3. Consider the context: "the beginning of the creation of (by) God" is a title given to Jesus by John and is not explained by the context surrounding Revelation 3:14.

4. Consider other Scriptures that would support a view: John 1:3, *"All things came into existence through him . . ."* and Colossians 1:16, *"because by means of him all [other] things were created in the heavens and upon the earth . . ."* (NWT).59. These verses support Jesus as Creator and would justify understanding Revelation 3:14's description of Jesus as the originating source of creation. "Ruler" is also justified since *arche* is frequently used in the political sense.

Bottom Line: The Greek word for "beginning," *arche,* is used in several ways. In John 1:1 it means the "beginning of time." In Colossians 1:16 it means a "ruler." In Revelation 3:14 arche can be used in a passive sense (he was created), or in an active sense (he was creating). The context provides no clue to what he means. So we look at other Scriptures. John 1:3 and Colossians 1:16 clearly speak of Jesus as Creator and justify taking arche in the active sense. Unless the JW's can give you any Scriptures that clearly speak of Jesus being created, they cannot use this verse as proof that he was.

II. Proverbs 8:22ff: "Jehovah himself produced me as the beginning of his way, the earliest of his achievements of long ago." NWT

JW Interpretation: Verse 12 identifies "wisdom" as the one speaking in this passage. "Wisdom" is Jesus who says he was "produced" by God and became his "master worker" (vs. 30). He was involved in the creation process, after he himself was created since he was "the earliest of his achievements."

Refutation: This is not Jesus. Reading from other verses one will understand that Solomon is using personification of wisdom in order to make reading enjoyable. For example, chapter 7:4-5 says, *Say to wisdom: "You are my sister;" and may you call understanding itself "Kinswoman," to guard you against the woman stranger, against the foreigner who has made her own sayings smooth."* Was Jesus a woman? No! In Proverbs 8, Solomon is telling his readers that if God used the quality of wisdom to create the universe, think of how it can be used in your own life for avoiding pitfalls and being successful at your endeavors. Wisdom, therefore, is not referring to Jesus.

The Personal Work

Bottom Line: The New Testament writers never employ Proverbs 8 in reference to Jesus. If "Wisdom" in Proverbs 8 is in fact "Jesus," who is "Shrewdness" in verse 1 and "Discernment" in verse 12? Finally, referring to Jesus in this passage is both out of place and goes against what Solomon is trying to teach. Solomon is not referring to Jesus in Proverbs 8, but is simply using a figure of speech called personification, as he does throughout Proverbs in order to be creative.

III. John 3:16: "For God loved the world so much that he gave his only-begotten Son . . ."

JW Interpretation: Only-begotten" means Jesus was begat or given birth by God. So he had a beginning.

Refutation: "Only-begotten," therefore, means "unique," "chosen," "special," or "exalted" in some sense.66 The Greek word for "only-begotten" in Hebrews 11:17 is the same word used in John 3:16. The JW may respond, "But, 'begotten' signifies a beginning to existence." Ask if it does in Hebrews 11:17. So we still have no Scripture that indicates Jesus was created.

Bottom Line: In John 3:16, "only-begotten" does not mean "only-born," but special in some sense as indicated by Isaac being called Abraham's "only-begotten" son in Hebrews 11:17 in spite of Ishmael being Abraham's son as well.

IV. Colossians 1:15: "He is the image of the invisible God, the firstborn of all creation."

JW Interpretation: Jesus was the first thing created by God.

Refutation: The Greek word for "firstborn" is *prototokos*. It appears throughout both the Old Testament (Septuagint) and the New Testament with different shades of meaning:
  A. Chronological: Emphasis is on the order of birth (Genesis 10:15; 19:30-31; Exodus 13:15).
  B. Positional: Emphasis is on the position of being the firstborn, with all of the honor and favor that is due to one being born first (Psalm 89:27, Col.1:15-18).

Jesus is "firstborn" in a positional sense, and this verse may not be used as a text in support of the view that Jesus was created. If anything, it points to the deity of Christ. Therefore, we still have no Scriptures that indicate Jesus was created.

Bottom Line: The word "firstborn" can be used in a chronological sense (first to be born or first created) or in a positional sense (one who has the honor and rights of a firstborn son [Ps. 89:27; Jer. 31:9]). We are fortunate that Paul explains what he means by "firstborn" in the verses that follow. Paul says Jesus is the Creator of the universe, Sustainer of the universe, Head of the Church, Risen Lord and, therefore, Chief of all things. This only points to the positional sense, not the chronological.

V. John 14:28: ". . . the Father is greater than I am."

JW Interpretation: "How can Jesus be God when He says, "The Father is greater than I am?"

Refutation: Jesus may be referring to his incarnate position, not his essence. The biblical standard is that the husband is, as positioned, greater than the wife in the home, yet both he and his wife are equal in essence. As the wife voluntarily submits herself to her husband, the Son voluntarily submits himself to the Father.

Bottom Line: When Jesus said the Father was greater than himself, he was referring to the Father's position, not his essence.

VI. Passages where the Father is called the God of Jesus (Mk 15:34; Jn. 20:17; Eph. 1:3, 17) or where God is referred to being distinct from Jesus (Jn. 17:3).

JW Interpretation: Both the New Testament writers and Jesus himself called the Father the God of Jesus on several occasions. If Jesus was God, why would he call the Father his God?

Refutation: This is the most difficult argument to answer of all the reasons provided by the Watchtower to support their view of Jesus.

    A. The New Testament writers, particularly John and Paul, clearly say Jesus is God and refer to the Father as the God of Jesus ((Jn. 1:1; 20:17, 28; Rev.22:13, Eph. 1:3; Col. 2:9).)So there was a sense in which they understood these two beliefs to be compatible.

The Personal Work

B. The Earliest Church Fathers, particularly Ignatius and Polycarp, clearly call Jesus "God," and also refer to the Father as the God of Jesus. Just like the New Testament writers, they did not appear to see a tension between the two.

C. The Father may be God to Jesus in the sense that he is the final authority to Jesus. Verses such as John 1:1 and Colossians 2:9 clearly speak of Jesus having the same essence of deity that the Father has. Nevertheless, Jesus submits to the Father who is his final authority.

Bottom Line: Jesus referred to the Father as his God. This does not mean Jesus himself was not God, for the Apostles and the earliest Church fathers all recognized him as God while at the same time recognizing that the Father was Jesus' God with no apparent tension. Furthermore, the Father may be God to Jesus in the sense that he is his final authority before whom unswerving and unquestioned love and devotion are given above all others.

15.
BIBLICAL TEXTS FOR THE DEITY OF CHRIST

This chapter examines five biblical texts that strongly support the doctrine that Jesus is God. These texts are what bring up the concept of Trinity as studied by the third century theologians.

1. Isaiah 9:6: "For a child will be born to us, a son will be given to us; and the government will rest on His shoulders; and His name will be called Wonderful Counselor, Mighty God, Eternal Father, and Prince of Peace."

Christians understand this verse to be a

prophecy about the coming Messiah. Jesus is here referred to as "Mighty God." The original Hebrew is not at all comparative in this verse.

a) ***Almighty God*** is the Hebrew ***El Shaddai.*** "The idea behind the root in Akkadian and in Hebrew seems to be that of impelling force, hence, the sovereign, 'Almighty God.'"84 The translation, "Almighty God," is from the Septuagint.

b) ***Mighty God*** is the Hebrew ***El Gibbor,*** and can be translated "God, the hero or champion among the army. It means a God who is mighty or superior, strong, brave, valiant, a hero. These Hebrew words have different, unrelated meanings. "Mighty God" does not stand inferior to "Almighty God" as the term, "strong," stands inferior to "strongest." They are unrelated terms, as in "brilliant" and "strong."

Bottom Line: Isaiah calls Jesus, "God." The Watchtower's attempts to explain this by claiming "mighty God" is less than "almighty God" reveals a lack of knowledge of the Hebrew language because the words "mighty" and "almighty" are not comparative in meaning, and Isaiah calls the Father "mighty God" one chapter later.

2. John 20:28: "Thomas answered and said to him: 'My Lord and my God!'"

This is a difficult verse for the JW because it is so clear. The JW will respond that either Thomas said, "My Lord" to Jesus, then looked heavenward and said, "My God!" However, there are four reasons why the Watchtower response is inadequate:

1) "Thomas answered and said to him: 'My Lord and my God!" He was addressing Jesus.

2) In Psalm 35:23 (Septuagint), the same Greek grammatical structure is used as in John 20:28, 'My Lord and my God' David was addressing one person.

3) Jesus never rebuked Thomas for calling him "God."

4) It is unlikely that Thomas, a pious Jew who was accustomed to carefully guarding his lips, would take the Lord's name in vain, especially when he saw the risen Jesus.

Bottom Line: Thomas addresses Jesus as his God. Attempts by the Watchtower to explain

The Personal Work

this by claiming Thomas was looking heavenward when he said "my God" or that he just uttered the statement as an expression of surprise fails to carefully observe Thomas' statement "to him," the similar Greek grammatical structure in Psalm 35:23, that Jesus never rebuked Thomas for calling him God, and the fact that the pious Jew, Thomas, would be unlikely to take the Lord's name in vain.

3. Colossians 2:9: *"for in him all the fullness of deity dwells in bodily form.* "The New World Translation renders "divine quality" instead of "deity." The two Greek words are *1) "theotetos"* one who occupies the divine office and possesses all divine power. The emphasis is on his nature. *2) Theiotetos:* divinity or has the quality of the divine; that which shows God to be God, and gives Him the right to worship. The emphasis is on his attributes.

Both acknowledge the deity of Christ. But the latter, *theotetos,* is stronger and is the word Paul uses. All the fullness of God's essence dwells in Christ in bodily form. Thus, Colossians 2:9 clearly refers to Jesus as God.

Bottom Line: The Greek word Paul uses for "deity" means Jesus is in essence God.

4. God and Jesus are both referred to as the:
     a) Alpha and Omega,
     b) First and Last,
     c) Beginning and End.
   A. God: Rev. 21:6, Is. 44:6
   B. Jesus: Rev. 1:8, 17-18; 2:8, 22:13

Bottom Line: Since John addresses Jesus and God interchangeably throughout these passages, it is clear he viewed Jesus as God. This is strengthened further by our fifth text, which is also from John.

5 John 1:1: "In the beginning was the Word, and the Word was with God, and the Word was God."
John 1:14 tells us that "the Word" is Jesus. Therefore, when John states in the third clause of verse 1 that "the Word was God," he claims that Jesus is God in the plainest of terms. JWs claim that the final clause should be translated "the Word was a god" (NWT).

The Watchtower has taken a few statements out of context to justify their translation, *"the Word was a god,"* from an article, which states that their translation is wrong, and that Jesus possesses the nature of God. They also claim that here are many other Bible verses in which almost all translators in other languages consistently insert the article 'a' when translating Greek sentences with the same structure."

What Jehovah's Witnesses do not say is those proper names, places, and certain words such as "God," "Lord," and "Holy Spirit" appear numerous times throughout the New Testament with and without the article, with no apparent change of meaning and are, therefore, exempt from the very general rule of when to insert the indefinite article 'a' when translating Greek.

Some other arguments Jehovah's Witnesses use

1. "The word 'Trinity' is not found in the Bible." Trinity is the term we use to describe the Godhead, one in essence but three persons. The question is not what we call it, but if the concept is taught in Scripture "theology."

2. "The concept of the 'Trinity' has pagan origins before Jesus." There are many other stories in the Bible that have pagan origin. This does not mean it is not true about Christianity. Even if the concept of a Trinity preceded Christianity, it would not prove Christianity copied it from other religions.

3. "If Jesus is God, then he prayed to himself in John 17." He prayed to the Father, another person of the Godhead, to whom he submits. The difference is in position, not essence.

Further More
Multiple biblical figures viewed Jesus as God; Isaiah, John, Thomas, and Paul. Although Jesus is never recorded as proclaiming, "I am God," His actions and claims spoke very loud. He accepted worship (Matthew 14:25-33; 28:8-10; John 9:35-38). The question we need to ask then is "Did Jesus do anything that would indicate that he thought of himself as God? "By considering the fact that he accepted worship that he knew was only for God, claimed to have authority over God's Law, and spoke using his own authority, it seems clear that Jesus did think of himself as God.

THE PERSONAL WORK

16.
DEALING WITH MORMONS

The Church of Christ of the Latter-day Saints, as they are commonly called, started in 1830 by Joseph Smith who claimed to have received the message from Jesus Christ, God, and angel Moroni. They have four sources of authority: the Bible, the Book of Mormon, the Pearl of Great Price, and Doctrine and Covenants.

It is one of the fastest growing churches in America, other European countries, and some parts of Africa, especially South Africa. However, it has found its roots in the central and southern parts of Africa. Today, the Mormons are divided into two major groups, The Church of Jesus Christ of Latter-day Saints (the Mormons), and The Reorganized Church of Jesus Christ of Latter Day Saints.

Doctrine of the Mormons
Mormon beliefs are fundamentally different from Biblical Christianity. For example, for Mormons:

- God was once a human as we are now, and progressed to become God. He is one of many Gods.
- Man has the ability to progress and become a god just as Jehovah did.
- Jesus is the son of God, but not part of the Godhead. Mormons do not believe in the Trinity
- Polygamy was being greatly advocated, only to be discouraged later.
- The Bible is not in its original status, it has been distorted by some writers, hence the giving of the Book of Mormons by Christ Jesus.

The Mormonism has four sources that they consider to be Scripture: the Bible, the Book of Mormon, the Pearl of Great Price, and Doctrine and Covenants. The Pearl of Great

Price contains the Book of Moses, the Book of Abraham, and the Writings of Joseph Smith.

Mormons' Approach
Mormons are wonderful people who are very sincere about their faith and are very caring. Although Mormon scholars are well aware of the challenges which face them, Mormon laity's, including Mormon missionaries, are pretty much in the dark.

Like the Jehovah's Witnesses, the Mormons will first seek to find common ground with you on many of the Christian doctrines. Then they will begin to twist the doctrine to suit their wits. They tell you that Joseph Smith replaced the apostles to bring restoration after the apostasy of the church. Thus, the Church of Jesus Christ of Latter-day Saints is the true Church for they bring restoration.

However, every Christian worker should understand that Mormons are not enemies, and never to be treated as one. We have to love and pray for them. Here are some suggestions to bear in mind when talking to the Mormons:

1. Set the agenda
However they approach you let them know that you are satisfied with being a Christian, but is open-minded and would like to discuss some issues concerning their beliefs that are bothersome to you.

2. Establish that the Bible is reliable.
Take the time to show them that the Bible is trustworthy. This gives them a solid place to go when they leave the Mormon Church.

3. Discuss the challenges to the Book of Mormon posed by archaeology and history.
This point in particular destroys the credibility of Joseph Smith. If Smith's translation of the Book of Abraham is completely wrong, then there is no reason to believe his translation of the Book of Mormon is any better.

4. Demonstrate that feelings can be misleading and actually prove nothing.
Show yourself to be a loving and knowledgeable Christian. The object is not to win an argument but to try to lead a sincere person to the truth. Therefore, present the evidence in a patient and loving manner.

Christianity is trustworthy because the text of the *Bible* is pure and much of it is confirmed by archaeology and secular history. There is no confirmation of the *Book of Mormon* from archaeology or history. Encourage the Mormons with whom you are sharing to pray and think about their personal situation. It is their souls that are on the line.

Answering the Mormons
Mormons are well equipped to answer many of the issues Christians bring to their attention and have answers adequate to silence the average critic. Although there are many issues, which you may bring to the Mormons' attention, focus on four (4) that are of primary importance:

1.   The Bible is Reliable: Mormons believe that the Bible is unreliable because it has been corrupted through numerous translations. The original words of the Bible have been preserved with remarkable purity and that its accuracy has been confirmed by both history and archaeology. They will only respond that the Bible is unreliable.

2. There is no archaeological confirmation of the Book of Mormon: There is no professional archaeological evidence to confirm Mormonism.

3. The Book of Abraham is a fraud: Joseph Smith purchased some ancient Egyptian papyri and claimed it was an original book penned by Abraham himself while in Egypt. The 1967 Professional Egyptologists' translations bear no resemblance to Smith's translation, exposing him as a charlatan.

4. **There is no Evidence for Mormonism:** There is no biblical evidence for the Mormons.

17.
FACTS AND EVIDENCE AGAINST MORMONS

1 The Bible is Reliable
It is necessary to first demonstrate to the Mormons that the Bible is reliable and that its text is pure and undistorted. The Bible is a reliable document that has been accurately preserved over thousands of years. Archaeology and secular history confirms the accuracy of the Bible.

A. The New Testament: Thousands of ancient manuscripts, ancient versions, and quotations of the New Testament found in the writings of the early Church Fathers provide evidence that the New Testament we have today was what was written in original Greek.

1. Greek Manuscripts: Approximately 5,000 manuscripts of the New Testament have survived in the original language.

2. Ancient Versions. By the second century, the New Testament was being translated into different languages which provide ground for comparison.

3. Early Church Fathers. Within 300 years of Christ, almost 36,000 quotations of the New Testament appear in the writings of the early Church Fathers.

B. The Old Testament: The Old Testament was written in Hebrew before the New Testament (between 1400-400 B. C.). One issue on which Mormons, Jehovah's Witnesses, and Christians agree is Jesus and his apostles believed that the Old Testament was the inspired, uncorrupted Word of God.

Mormons believe that although Jesus and his apostles had God's Word in their hands, much of it has since been corrupted and, therefore, is not trustworthy. However, survey of the Masoretic text, the Dead Sea Scrolls, ancient versions, and Old Testament verses cited in the New Testament disproves such claims:

The Personal Work

1) Masoretic Text. The text of the Old Testament used by translators of the *Bible* is referred to as the Masoretic text meticulously copied and edited the text between A. D. 600-1000.

2) Dead Sea Scrolls. In 1946, hundreds of scrolls and fragments were found in eleven caves in northern Israel. Texts from every book of the Old Testament were found, with the lone exception of Esther. They all bear the same message.

3) Ancient Versions. Two ancient versions are helpful when comparing them to the Hebrew text: 1) The Septuagint was the Greek translation of the Old Testament used in Jesus' day and is quoted many times by the New Testament writers. 2) The Samaritan Pentateuch is the first five books of the Bible which were used by the Samaritans, a group of Jews which permanently separated themselves from the general Jewish population around 500 B. C. they have striking similarities to the Masoretic text.

4) Old Testament verses in the New Testament. The writers of the New Testament cite verses from the Old Testament a total of 330 times. They have an incredible correlation to the Old Testament that we have today.

2 There is *no* specific confirmation of the *Book of Mormon* from archaeology.

A. What Mormon archeologists say?

Most of these Mormonism practicing archaeologists have honestly revealed that they have never at any point found any archaeological evidence pertaining to the Book of Mormons. Brigham Young University (BYU) is owned by the Mormons. None of its archaeologists has ever given the evidence for the Book of Mormons.

B What non-Mormon archeologists say?

Every statement from the Smithsonian Institution is damaging to the Book of Mormons as far as archaeological findings are concerned. For example, the Smithsonian Institution has never used the Book of Mormon in any way as a scientific guide because they see no direct connection between the archeology of the New World and the subject matter of the book.

Therefore, there is a consensus from professional archaeologists, Mormon and non-

Mormon alike, that there is no specific confirmation of the Book of Mormon from archaeology. This is something damaging.

C The Claims of the Mormons

A.   The *Book of Mormon* claims that the ancient inhabitants spoke and wrote in "Reformed Egyptian" and Hebrew. However, there are no artifacts with writings in these languages in this regard.

B.   The *Book of Mormon* states that the two peoples mentioned (Nephites and Lamanites) had Jewish beliefs that became Christian when the resurrected Christ appeared to them. However, there is no evidence that the ancient inhabitants in the Americas had either Jewish or Christian beliefs.

C.   Joseph Smith claimed that when Moroni appeared to him, he was told that Moroni's father, Mormon, buried the gold plates upon which the *Book of Mormon* was based on the hill Cumorah just before the great final battle there (Mormon 6:6). Great battles had been fought near hill Cumorah with casualties left unburied. But nothing has ever been found at hill Cumorah to prove these claims.

3 The Book of Abraham is a fraud

Among the four books used by the Mormons, the book of Abraham is the most used along the Book of Mormons. However, there are many problems regarding this book contrary to the claims by the Mormons. For example, the translations of the Egyptologists which included John Wilson Klaus Baer and Richard Parker could not either confirm Joseph Smith as a true prophet or convict him as a charlatan.

John Wilson discovered that the text Smith used to translate the Book of Abraham was actually "a related mortuary text of late times, the so-called Book of the Breathing which was being buried with the dead to be a guide at life after death. Wilson also claimed that one of the drawings Smith included in the *Book of Abraham* was actually a hypocephalus, "a cartonnage disk which was placed under the head of a mummy toward the end of ancient Egyptian history. All the other two concur with Parker in this regard.

It is, however, said that Smith might have obtained his source from his Jewish teacher, Professor Joshua Seixas; it was certainly not a miraculous knowledge. Some prominent

Mormons claim that *Genesis Apocryphon,* the *Dead Sea Scrolls* and the *Book of Enoch* have many parallels to the *Book of Abraham* and, thus, confirm that Joseph Smith received the translation of the *Book of Abraham* through divine inspiration, because he could not have possibly known these accounts in his day. However, careful study on this claim shows only weak parallels are available. The *Book of Abraham* problem remains a death knell for Mormonism.

4. Feelings are often inaccurate

While Mormon scholars admit valid challenges to Mormonism from archaeology and the *Book of Abraham,* they say the evidences of Mormonism's truthfulness is the Book of Mormon itself, God's confirmation in your spirit, and the number of changed lives. They say that we do not need evidence to support its truthfulness because God has already confirmed in their hearts that it is true. This belief is extremely difficult to overcome when talking to your Mormon friends. However, there is no sufficient evidence provided by Mormons for Mormonism's truth.

It is possible for someone to feel confident that they are okay in their relationship with

God but in reality are not (Matthew 7:21-22). Mormons are not exceptional. Islam makes the same claims and yet Mormons do not regard the *Qur'an* or Islamic doctrine as being divinely inspired. One can be sincere and confident that God has shown them the way and still be mistaken, as is the case with Muslims. The only way to determine the true source is to look at outside evidence.

The Old Testament leaders encouraged people to remember what God did for them. The New Testament leaders "reasoned" from the Scriptures (Acts 17:2; 18:4, 19) and offered proof, namely Jesus' resurrection (Acts 9:22; 17:31). No one just ever suggested.

At one point the Mormons will appeal to universalism, "Every sincere person will make it to Heaven, regardless of their beliefs." However, it is not compatible with biblical doctrine. The biblical view of faith is that it is always a trusting commitment based on known fact. There are three (3) types of faith to which men hold on: 1) Faith with evidence. This is reasonable faith, 2) Faith with no evidence, for or against. This is blind faith, and

3) Faith in spite of evidence against it. This is stubborn faith. Mormons belong to the third type.

18.
EVANGELIZING TO THE ROMAN CATHOLICIST

Many will ask why I have included the Roman Catholicity on the list of those to be evangelized. Are they not Christians? Are they not saved? Why now? Well, let us say that having already crossed my boundaries, this time, I have over-crossed it. But do not judge me before you read some of the Roma Catholic doctrine. This will lead you to making a decision if we should remove or indeed, add them to the list.

When is a person a Christian?
A person is a Christian when he/she believes

The Personal Work

the Gospel of God, Jesus Christ and the Bible; when he/she repents of sin and has faith alone in Christ alone for justification. The Gospel to be believed is that personal sinfulness is so deep that one cannot possibly go to heaven unless one has been given the righteousness of Jesus Christ. Unless one repents of sin and has full confidence in the sinless life and substitutionary finished work of Christ on the cross, he cannot be a Christian (Eph. 2:4-9; Rom.1:16-17). To concur with R.M Zins, a Christian believes that Christ's righteousness alone is the righteousness which enables God to save poor sinners. To believe less is a denial of the Gospel. To believe more is a denial of the Gospel.

Who then is a Roman Catholic?

A Roman Catholic is defined by the things which he believes about God, Jesus Christ and the Bible. A Roman Catholic is a person who places his/her trusts in the Roman Catholic religion's understanding of God, Jesus Christ and the Bible. Hence, a Roman Catholic believes in God, Jesus Christ and the Bible as presented and explained by the Roman Catholic authorities. That is where the difference begins between A Christian and a Catholic.

Roman Catholic and Salvation
Now, one can ask the two most important questions; "Can a Roman Catholic be a Christian?" The answer is "yes" if a Roman Catholic forsakes the Roman Catholic religion and believes the Gospel of God, Jesus Christ and the Bible. "Is Roman Catholicism a Christian religion?" The answer is "no." Roman Catholicism does not believe the Christian Gospel of God, Jesus Christ and the Bible.

The Differences
Things that we agree with the Roman Catholicism are not significant when compared with our vast differences:

I. Authority
Christians believe that the Bible alone is our authority (the 66 books of the Bible) -the Bible not only contains the Word of God but actually is the Word of God. We also believe in the formal sufficiency of the nibble –it can be readily understood in matters pertaining to Salvation and Sanctification. The Bible alone is the word of God. All Christians can know and understand what the Gospel of Salvation is and what the Lord requires of us for holy living through their own study of the Word of God.

The Personal Work

On the other hand, the Roman Catholics do not believe in only 66 books of the Bible. They have added the apocryphal books to the Bible. Also, the Roman Catholic does not believe that he/she is capable of understanding the Bible apart from the infallible teaching of the Roman Catholic authorities. The Roman Catholic authorities also add other sources of rule on an equal level with the Bible -Roman Catholic Tradition, the Magisterium (council that interprets the Bible and selects the Pope), and the Pope at Rome. Roman Catholics allow Rome to define and explain things pertaining to God, Jesus Christ and Salvation. It is a fatal mistake, forever setting Christians against Roman Catholicism.

The Message of Salvation
Christians believe that God has revealed in the Bible the Gospel of salvation. By believing the Gospel of salvation, Christians are assured of eternal life and are no longer under the wrath of God. There is therefore no condemnation for those who are in Christ Jesus.

The essence of the Gospel which guarantees salvation to all those who believe, is justification by faith alone in the finished work of Christ alone. Christians believe that there is a point in time where God opens one's heart to understand the Gospel of salvation and gives faith to believe the Gospel. The Christian vocabulary describing this event is called being born again or *born from above* (John 3:3).

Roman Catholics do not believe in a point- in-time Salvation. They do not believe in justification by faith alone in the finished work of Christ alone. Roman Catholics do not believe in a born again experience which makes one eternally secure and assured of heaven. For instance, Roman Catholics believe that water administered by a priest takes away the original sin of Adam. They also believe that justification is an ongoing process through the sacraments of the Roman Catholic religion.

Roman Catholics believe that participation in the Catholic Mass and the Catholic Penance brings about forgiveness of sins. Roman Catholics believe that personal holiness merits an increase in justification. Ultimately, the ground of justification in the Roman Catholic religion is not Christ's righteousness imputed to the poor sinner but rather good works done in faith.

The Person of Jesus Christ

Christians believe that Jesus Christ was truly God and truly man. Christians believe that there are Three Persons in One God - God the Father, Jesus Christ and the Holy Ghost - who are one in essence but different in personality. So do Roman Catholics. However, Christians do not believe that Jesus Christ can be called out of heaven and transformed into a piece of bread and a vial of wine. The doctrine of transubstantiation is abhorrent to Christians. Christians do not believe that the death of Jesus Christ must be re-presented on an un-bloody altar for the forgiveness of sins.

The Roman Catholics believe that Jesus Christ is transubstantiated into the wine and bread of the Roman altar where His death at Calvary is re-presented on an un-bloody altar for the forgiveness of sins. This is the essence of the Roman Catholic Mass.

Paraphernalia

Christian's have confidence in the promise of Christ. All who believe in Him have eternal life (Jn.3:16, 36; 5:24; 6:40, 47; Acts 13:48, Rom. 6:23; 1Jn. 5:13). Believing in Jesus

Christ means believing that being acquitted from sin is a free gift. Both believing too little and believing too much in Jesus is not a guarantee for eternity. For example, one can believe that Jesus was a good man or a prophet and an example and still be lost.

Also, to believe that Jesus came and preached a gospel to the Tonga of Malawi, that Jesus is a spirit brother of Lucifer, that Jesus is Michael the Archangel or that Jesus is contained in a piece of bread and sacrificed afresh on an altar is to present another Jesus.

Only one Jesus is the savior and only one gospel is the real Gospel. Ultimately, to believe in Jesus is not to have confidence in what Jesus makes of you rather that we believe that God accepts us for what Christ did for us.

The Bottom line

Starting with the wrong Authority and ending up with the wrong gospel message and presenting a different Jesus eliminates Roman Catholicism from Christianity. It also leads to a variety of teachings which openly contradict the tenants of Christian Faith, few of which are that:

The Personal Work

1. Rome believes in purgatory. There is no such place as Purgatory in Christian theology or in the Bible.

2. Rome believes in Indulgences which are said to reduce time spent suffering in Purgatory for sins committed on earth. There is no such thing as Indulgences in Christian theology or in the Bible.

3. Rome believes in the Immaculate Conception, Sinless Life, Assumption and Co-Redemptress status of Mary. There is no hint of this adulation of Mary in Christian theology or in the Bible.

4. Rome believes in the Infallibility of the Pope at Rome when he speaks on matters of faith and morals. There is no suggestion of this dictatorial position in Christian theology or in the Bible.

5. Rome believes in salvation within her religious procedures and believes as well that other non-Christian religions offer God's salvation to their faithful adherents. But, there is no place in Christian theology for salvation in non-Christian religions including Roman Catholicism, Mormonism, Buddhism, Hinduism, Je-

hovah Witnesses, Judaism, Muslims and all other religions outside of the Gospel of Christ.

Conclusion

It is deep error for Roman Catholics to think that they can call themselves Christians while *denying* the critical essentials of what the Bible teaches about the Gospel. It would be equally foolish for Christians to think that anyone can be a Christian while believing all that Roman Catholics believe. One is right and the other is wrong.

R.M Zins emphatically says that this is not a matter of semantics. It is not a matter of feelings. It is not a matter of opinion. It is not a matter of perception. It is not a matter of agreeing to disagree on some minor points. It is not a matter of definition of terms. It is not a matter of theological hair-splitting. It is not a matter of accepting those that differ. It is strictly a matter of truth and error. It is a matter of right thinking and wrong thinking. It is a matter of right believing and wrong believing. Catholics must be preached to for salvation.

The Personal Work

How to go about it?

1. Win the Catholic to trust the Scriptures as the only reliable authority on faith, and to believe that they can understand it.

2. Support everything you say with Bible verses.

3. Get the Catholic to pray with you that God will open his eyes to understand His word.

4. Share the Gospel with Him, as you would with any person but do it in such a way that you let the

5. Scriptures speak for itself. Take time to give the proper definition of theological terms.

6. If he is knowledgeable enough to be able to quote Bible verses that support his view, then offer to look up those verses on the spot and examine their context.

7. Bring up some provoking facts, to convince him that the RC church can no longer be considered as belonging to Christ (e.g. The RCC doctrine of Purgatory is backed by only one verse in

the Apocrypha)

8. Give your own testimony of how you became a Christian emphasizing the role of God's Word in your salvation.

9. Challenge the Catholic to discover God's truths for himself by carefully reading the Bible, and believing only what God says through it.

19.
TIPS FOR A PERSONAL WORKER

There are several things a Personal worker must learn and know from and about his Work. The Bible has full of example to such things so as to help us better understand the type of works we are called to.

A. Lessons for a Personal Worker

Acts 5:17-39 shows us some important lessons each Personal worker must learn and prepare for as he/she engages in God's service. In my over twenty years' experience as a worker, I have learned a great deal of lessons, sometimes in failure, sometimes in success. However, one thing I am happy about is that I have learned the best of lesson from it. Our passage here explains better several lessons I have also learned. I put forward seven important lessons from this passage:

1. Wherever God is working, the devil will also be at work (verse 17-18)
It was the devil working behind the apostles' persecution. If God is doing something, look out for Satan. It was so with Nehemiah when he was rebuilding the broken walls of Jerusalem. He faced opposition from within and without. We have to resist Satan and he will flee from us (Jas.4:7).

2. It is always safe to trust God where we are doing His will (18-19)
There are thousands of Christians in the world prison today. Thousands are being persecuted in Asian and other Arab nation prisons because they sought to be faithful to their Lord Jesus Christ. But there is no prison so dark, so strong that God cannot visit his people in it. The only important thing to do in such circumstance is to trust God (Ps.37:5-6). Remember Daniel's three friends who kept on trusting even at appoint of death by fire (Dan.3:16-18). The blood of the Lamb and testimony or confession of our

THE PERSONAL WORK

mouth will quench the fiery furnaces of the enemy (Rev.12:11)

3. We may still believe and rejoice in the ministry of Angels
Angels are our ministering spirits (Heb. 1:14). We are given ministry beyond that of the angels who wait orders from God. We do not need God to tell us again to go minister to a sinner. He had already given us the mandate and ministry.

4. We should obey God rather than men (Verse 32)
In spite of threats, imprisonments, and withdrawals of certain privileges, we must determine to go on preaching and doing God's work.

5. God gives the Holy Spirit to those who obey Him (verse 32)
The Holy Spirit is given to us as we obey the word of God (Acts 2:37-29). When we totally surrender to the Lord, in complete obedience, He fills us with the Holy Spirit. We must totally surrender to God all that we are, and have.

6. Recognize your partnership with God

To be effective for the Lord of Glory, we must recognize our partnership with the Holy Spirit (Verse 32). Peter and John recognized their partnership with the Holy Spirit in witnessing about Jesus.

7. When God initiates a work, He will prosper and complete it (verse 38)

Whatever God starts will never be overthrown. If your work is started by God in you, it will surely come to pass. The church was started by God, and it shall never fall as others claim. Christ will never fail, and He is the builder of the church – al will be well (Phil.1:16).

B. The "Do Not's" For the Christian Worker

In as much as we may use any other means to win soul's, there are other things that a Christian worker should NOT dare to do in whatever work or ministry as he is dealing with the clients or inquirers.

1) Do not act familiar with those of opposite sex (1 Thess. 5:22). Avoid any appearance of evil.

2) Do not pray long prayers as you are directing a seeker (Dan.9:20)

THE PERSONAL WORK

3) Do not look at any case as being hard (1 Tim. 1:15). Trust the accomplishing power of the Holy Spirit.

4) Do not be discouraged when seeker's response seems negative. Leave results with God (1 Pet. 5:8-9)

5) Do not discuss church conditions or Christian failure with seekers? They know those things (1 Pet.2:21)

6) Do not wait for an impression (2 Tim.4:2), but leave an impact.

7) Do not argue with the inquirer (Mt.7:6), but help him/her to know the truth.

8) Do not attempt to prove truth or spiritual things (Isa.55:10-11)

9) Do not always try to explain all spiritual things (2 Cor.2:14)

10) Do not be in a habit of telling own experience- point the inquirer to Jesus (2 Tim.2:15, 4:2).

11) Do not exalt self above the sinner (1 Cor. 9:19-23)

12) Do not overwork the pronoun 'I', exalt Christ Jesus (Jn.16:13-16).

13) Do not give scriptures you are not sure of or from a 'hear-say'. Have the Bible handy (Rom.3:4).

14) Do not hurry over a scripture. Em-

phasize what is needful (2 Cor. 13:1)

15) Do not raise unnecessary objections. An inquirer will do this (2 Tim.2:15)

16) Do not condemn sinners who already stand condemnation before God (Jn.3:16-21)

17) Do not insist on going to the altar or place of worship (do not start by invite a sinner to church), but rather insist on immediate surrender (2 Cor.6:2)

18) Do not dwell on sin and sinners bad habit, dwell on the love and grace of God for them (2 Cor.5:17).

19) Do not give too many points at a time (Mt.10:16)

20) Do not permit the inquirer to lead you from one subject to another for the sake of argument (2 Ti. 2:25)

21) Do not state your ideas or beliefs. Give what God's word says (Jn.16:11-17)

22) Do not act victoriously or proud when you score a point (Gal.2:13)

23) Do not be led to side issues (Jn.3:3-5)

24) Do not tell sad stories. Point the sinner to Christ's love (Jn.3:16)

25) Do not cross a seeker with non-essential things. If you do not agree with him

say nothing (Pr.11:30)

26) Do not talk all the times. Answer the inquirer wisely (1 Pet. 3:15)

27) Do not leave one case for another unless you are through with it (Mt.1:16-20)

28) Do not talk too loud or get excited. Be calm and prayerful (Jn.3:1-13)

29) Do not be over-zealous or force anyone to follow Christ (Mt. 7:6, 10:16).

30) Do not intrude. This may confuse the inquirer and worker (1 Cor. 14:40)

31) Do not be indifferent to those seeking God; do not hinder those working please (1 Tim. 3:15)

32) Do not interrupt any worker. Conversation can fail (Rom.13:10)

33) Do not crowd around a seeker. This may embarrass or confuse him (1 Cor. 14:40)

34) Do not tell the seeker to think it over. Bring to a decision at once if possible (Mt. 13:19, 2 Cor.6:2)

35) Do not have bad breath or noticeable body odor (1 Cor.6:19-20)

36) Do not be a hypocritical (Rom. 2:21-24)

37) Do not hurry the seeker if he wants to pray (Lk.13:1-5; 18:13-14)

38) Do not tell persons they are saved.

Let the Holy Spirit bear witness (1 Jn.1:9, Rom.8:16)

39) Do not insist keeping the sinners on their knees. Pray with them while sitting or standing (Lk.18:9-14)

40) Do not let an inquirer go away unsatisfied or doubtful. Persuade them to have faith in God (Eph.2:8-9)

41) Do not insist that an inquirer get saved the same way you did. Circumstances change (Jn.3:16)

42) Do not emphasize emotion; faith first, feelings later (Eph.2:8-9)

43) Do not lean on an inquirer. Their burdens are already heavy enough (Jn.16:8)

44) Do not act indifferent to any human need (Rom.12:11). Help if you can.

45) Do not be discourteous, or make a seeker think he is untouchable (Mt. 11:19). Wisdom justifies the way.

46) Do not try to force anyone to accept the Bible as God's word (Mt.7:6).

47) Do not lose patience with weak people (Gal. 5:22-23). Let the fruit of the Spirit in you manifest

48) Do not be careless or half-hearted in dealing with men. Eternal souls are at stake (Lk.19:10)

49) Do not lose sight of the value of a

soul. Jesus died that each man might live (Mk.8:32, Jn.3:16, 1 Cor.6:20). No one is too sinful to be saved.

50) Do not fail to instruct a new convert regarding how to live successful Christian life (see 'How to live a Christian life, chapter 3, section B)

Primary Source References

- Billy Graham Christian Worker's Handbook © 1984, 1996 Billy Graham Evangelistic Association
- Christian Equippers International, the Biblicist P.O. Box 519 Springfield, Oregon 97477
- Christian Witness Among Muslims. Ghana, W. Africa: Africa Christian Press, 1971
- Dencher, Ted. The Watch Tower versus the Bible. Chicago: Moody Press, 1961
- Dr. Ergun Caner; Ankerberg Theological Research Institute, PO Box 8977 - Chattanooga, TN 37414 USA 423-892-772

- Finis Jennings Dake, Dake's Annotated Reference Bible, Dake's Bible Sales Inc. P.O. Box 1050 Lawrenceville, Georgia 3024
- Goldsmith, Martin. Islam and Christian Witness. Downers Grove: Intervarsity Press, 1982.
- Lorri MacGregor; MacGregor Ministries, Box 454 Metaline Falls WA 99153,
- Phil Roberts; Southern Baptist Convention, Copyright 2015 North American Mission Board, SBC
- R.A Torrey, How to work for Christ, A Compendium of Effective methods, Book 1.
- Reasons to Believe in the Bible. http://ourdailybread.org
- Rex Yancey, Characteristics of a Christian Worker, Salem Church Products
- Rich Deem: Jehovah's Witnesses Beliefs Compared to Christianity;
- Tom Walker, Outreach, Inc.,
- Walter Martin, The kingdom of the Cults: Bethany House Publishers; 11400 Hampshire Avenue South Bloomington, Minnesota 55438.

- Finis Jennings Dake, Dake's Annotated Reference Bible, Dake's Bible Sales Inc. P.O. Box 1050 Lawrenceville, Georgia 3024
- Goldsmith, Martin. Islam and Christian Witness. Downers Grove: Intervarsity Press, 1982.
- Lorri MacGregor; MacGregor Ministries, Box 454 Metaline Falls WA 99153,
- Phil Roberts; Southern Baptist Convention, Copyright 2015 North American Mission Board, SBC
- R.A Torrey, How to work for Christ, A Compendium of Effective methods, Book 1.
- Reasons to Believe in the Bible. http://ourdailybread.org
- Rex Yancey, Characteristics of a Christian Worker, Salem Church Products
- Rich Deem: Jehovah's Witnesses Beliefs Compared to Christianity;
- Tom Walker, Outreach, Inc.,
- Walter Martin, The kingdom of the Cults: Bethany House Publishers; 11400 Hampshire Avenue South Bloomington, Minnesota 55438.